THEMATIC UNIT
Slavery

Written by Krista Warnock-Carman

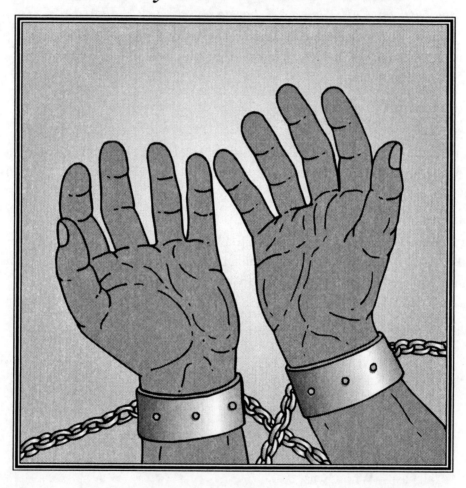

Teacher Created Resources, Inc.
6421 Industry Way
Westminster, CA 92683
www.teachercreated.com
©2000 Teacher Created Resources, Inc.
Reprinted, 2005
Made in U.S.A.
ISBN-1-57690-613-2

Edited by
Karen Tam Froloff

Illustrated by
Bruce Hedges

Cover Art by
Agi Palinay

Table of Contents

Introduction

Slavery is a riveting thematic unit that gives students the opportunity to learn about and experience slavery through the multiple intelligences. Its 80 pages contain literature-based activities in all subject areas. The content is challenging and will encourage students to re-evaluate the world around them.

Two literature selections will enable the students to work through the concept of slavery. *To Be A Slave* by Julius Lester and *Letters from a Slave Girl—The Story of Harriet Jacobs* by Mary Lyons are centered around activities that build upon the knowledge and concepts that are introduced in the books. To completely immerse the class in this theme, there are activities in language arts, social studies, math, science, art, music, and P.E. Completing this unit are culminating activities. These activities allow closure for the students to this intense theme.

The thematic unit includes the following:

❏ **Literature selections:** summaries of two books with related lessons that cross the curriculum

❏ **Planning guides:** suggestions for sequencing lessons each day of the unit

❏ **Curriculum connections:** activities for language arts, social studies, math, science, art, music, P.E., and technology

❏ **Group projects:** activities that encourage cooperative learning

❏ **Literature-related activities:** additional slavery-related books with activities

❏ **Enrichment activities:** some lessons are followed with enrichment ideas for topics that may be explored further

❏ **Culminating activities:** ideas that provide closure to the intense theme of slavery

❏ **Bibliography:** additional literature selections and slavery research books

❏ **Resource materials:** teacher books and technology sources that are helpful for additional research

---

To keep this valuable resource intact so that it can be used year after year, you may wish to punch holes in the pages and store them in a three-ring binder.

Introduction *(cont.)*

Why a Balanced Language Approach?

The strength of a balanced language approach is that it involves children in using all modes of communication—reading, writing, listening, observing, illustrating, and speaking. Communication skills are interconnected and integrated into lessons that emphasize the entirety of whole language rather than isolating its parts. The child reads, writes, speaks, listens, and thinks in response to a literature experience introduced by the teacher. In these ways language skills grow rapidly, stimulated by involvement and interest in the topic.

Why Thematic Planning?

One useful tool for implementing an integrated and balanced language program is thematic planning. By choosing a theme with correlating literature selections for a unit of study, a teacher can plan activities throughout the day that lead to cohesive, in-depth study of the topic. Students practice and apply their skills in meaningful contexts. Consequently, they tend to learn and retain more. Both teacher and students are freed from a day that is broken into unrelated segments of isolated drill and practice.

Why Cooperative Learning?

In addition to academic skills and content, students need to learn social skills. No longer can this area be taken for granted. Students must learn to work cooperatively in groups in order to function well in modern society. Group activities should be a regular part of school life, and teachers should consciously include social objectives as well as academic objectives in their planning. The teacher should clarify and monitor the qualities of good group interaction just as he or she would clarify and monitor the academic goals of a project.

There are four basic components of Cooperative Learning:

- All group members need to work together to accomplish the task.

- Groups should be heterogeneous.

- Activities need to be designed so that each student contributes to the group, and individual group members can be assessed on their performance.

- Groups need to know the social as well as the academic objectives of a lesson.

Slavery

Historical Background

"To be a slave. To be owned by another person, as a car, house, or table is owned. To live as a piece of property that could be sold—a child sold from its mother, a wife from her husband. To be a slave to know, despite the suffering and deprivation, that you were human, more human than he who said you weren't human. They were not slaves. They were people. Their condition was slavery."—Julius Lester

"Slavery," according to *Webster's New World Dictionary*, is: 1. The owning of slaves as practice. 2. The condition of a slave; bondage. 3. Drudgery; toil.

Slavery is in no way a new institution; it has been a part of human life since early times. In ancient Greece, Rome, Egypt, Mesopotamia, and Africa, people believed slavery was a natural part of society. Slavery in the New World began in the early 1600s when Spanish and Portuguese colonies in Mexico, Central and South America, and the Caribbean needed cheap labor.

In the beginning, Native Americans were used, but they were not believed to be hard workers and were not immune to the diseases of the Europeans and became quite ill and died. The Europeans discovered that Africans weren't as susceptible to disease and worked much harder. Spain and Portugal first established the African slave trade, and the Europeans joined in the lucrative business quickly. Slaves were captured and exported by African slave merchants who made a sizable profit, also.

Groups of captured Africans were bound together and marched to the coast where they were traded. Price was negotiated based on the health and physical condition of each slave. After the purchase, slaves were often branded with the mark of whoever funded the expedition. They were then put aboard a ship and forced to live for weeks in close confinement with little food or water until they reached their destination.

Africans who landed in the New World began a life of toil and drudgery. They had no rights and were treated like animals. They were often beaten, starved, and accused of hideous crimes. However, the African people were strong and never gave in to their desolate situation. They created a culture of music, art, and spirituality throughout America.

In 1777, Vermont was the first state to abolish slavery and more Northern states followed. However, in 1787, the United States Constitution was approved with three clauses that protected slavery. Slavery had become a part of the social structure in the South and therefore continued in the United States for many years until 1863.

As a result of the Civil War, Abraham Lincoln signed the Emancipation Proclamation which was written to free the slaves. However, it only applied to the Southern states that were occupied by the North. Freedom for all slaves didn't come until the end of the Civil War in 1865, and for some it was even later. Although the Emancipation Proclamation was a victory for over one million slaves, the battle was far from won. It would take many years for African Americans to gain rights, financial stability, and equality among all people. Many believe that African Americans are still fighting the battle today.

To Be A Slave

by Julius Lester

Book Summary

To Be A Slave explores slavery from the perspective of actual slaves. Julius Lester compiled stories, quotes, and anecdotes from former slaves and created a book that described slavery from the point of view of those who were there. A Newbery Honor Book, it contains the recollections of an African child being captured in his native land and his journey to the United States. There are stories of slave auctions and mothers being ripped apart from their children because they were sold to different masters. The memoirs of ex-slaves make the text come alive and allows one to experience slavery. The outline below is a suggested plan for using the various activities that are presented in this unit. You should adapt these to fit your own classroom situation.

Sample Plan

Lesson 1

❏ Make "Slavery Journals" (page 9).

❏ Read and discuss Chapter 1, "To Be a Slave."

❏ Discuss Historical Background (Setting the Stage, page 7, activity 1).

❏ Complete "Historical Research" (page 10).

❏ Discuss students' views on slavery ("Setting the Stage," page 7, activity 2).

Lesson 2

❏ Assign "Vocabulary Scramble" (page 11).

❏ Read Chapter 2, "The Auction Block."

❏ Complete "The Auction Block Discussion" (page 12).

❏ Discuss emotions ("Enjoying the Book," page 7, activity 2).

Lesson 3

❏ Read Chapter 3, "The Plantation."

❏ Complete "Describe the Plantation" (page 13).

❏ Discuss aspects of the plantation.

Lesson 4

❏ Read Chapter 4, "Resistance to Slavery–1."

❏ Complete the discussion ("Enjoying the Book," page 7, activity 4).

❏ Complete "Resistance to Slavery" (page 14).

❏ Assign "The Underground Railroad" (pages 36–39).

Lesson 5

❏ Complete "The Slaves' Social Life" (page 15).

❏ Read Chapter 5, "Resistance to Slavery–2."

❏ Discuss Frederick Douglass ("Extending the Book," page 8, activity 3).

❏ Assign "Anti-Slavery Speech" (page 16).

❏ Share speeches with the class and receive student feedback.

❏ Have book discussion ("Extending the Book", page 8, activity 4).

❏ Have students interview one another about their feelings toward slavery ("Extending the Book," page 8, activity 5).

Overview of Activities

Setting the Stage

1. Provide students with copies of the Historical Background—Slavery on page 5. Read and discuss together.

2. Read the "Prologue" of *To Be A Slave* by Julius Lester and facilitate a class discussion on slavery. Focus on the quotes from the slaves who were there and what they experienced. Ask students questions like: What do you know about slavery? How do you think it felt to be owned? What do you think of the slave's reaction to seeing white people for the first time? Discuss the accommodations on a slave ship and the chance of surviving the journey. If you were a slave, would you want to survive the journey if you knew the life that awaited you in the United States?

3. Have students make a slavery journal (page 9) to reflect upon future readings.

4. In order to understand the historical background of slavery, have the students research one of the topics and use the format found on page 10. Web sites may also be used to conduct research in this section (see Bibliography on pages 78–79). After the students complete the work sheet outline on page 10, they will write a three-paragraph essay following the format of the outline. Instruct them to use peer editing or teacher editing and then complete the final draft.

5. There will be some vocabulary in the book that may be unfamiliar to the students. To aid in their understanding, complete the Vocabulary Scramble on page 11.

Enjoying the Book

1. Read Chapter 2, "The Auction Block" and have students complete "The Auction Block Discussion" on page 12. Discuss with the students different emotions that are generated throughout the book. What emotions did the slaves' stories invoke in the students? How do they think they would be able to survive if they were slaves? At what points in the book did they feel disgust, sadness, anger, joy, hatred, etc.?

2. Read Chapter 3, "The Plantation" and complete "Describe the Plantation" on page 13.

3. Complete the activity "Who Owns…?" on page 69. This activity will give students a further understanding of the emotions and complexities of slavery.

4. Read Chapter 4, "Resistance to Slavery–1." Discuss with the class the differing views of the slaves and their masters. Why do they think this occurred? Which of these differences do the students believe are harmful? Do you think the masters used religion to control the slaves? Was this effective? Why or why not?

5. Complete the "Resistance to Slavery" questions on page 14. This page is useful for evaluation of the students' comprehension and can be treated as a quiz. The quiz should be given after this chapter has been read and discussed. Due to the detail of the questions, you may want to make it an open book quiz.

Overview of Activities *(cont.)*

Extending the Book

1. The slaves were allowed few social activities and were often punished for any socialization. Brainstorm with the class social activities in which the slaves may have been able to participate. Have the students complete "The Slaves' Social Life" on page 15 by choosing some of these activities and ranking them by preference. The questions that follow the ranking will assess their understanding of the slaves' social situation.

2. Have the students participate in the game "Bivoe Ebuma" on page 72. Ask the students to brainstorm what other types of games the slave children may have played. Ask the class to evaluate the suggested games as to their likelihood. Would the slaves probably have played a game like the one suggested? Why or why not?

3. The slaves in Chapter 5, "Resistance to Slavery–2," make mention of slaves that have escaped to freedom and others that helped with this process. Make copies of "Frederick Douglass" on page 49 available for students to read. Set aside time to discuss students' reactions to their readings.

4. Tell the students that they are part of an abolitionist, or anti-slavery, group that is appearing in front of the president to talk about why slavery is wrong. Have them complete the "Anti-Slavery Speech" on page 16.

5. Julius Lester worked hard to compile the stories of former slaves. Discuss as a class whether using the words and experiences of real slaves made the book more meaningful. Did the fact that it was about real people make slavery more real to you? Was it shocking to read that some horrible and disgusting things happened to real people? Was it more emotional to read knowing that these were the actual words spoken by a former slave?

6. Have the students interview one another about their reactions to slavery. Ask them if they learned anything new. Find out what shocked them most, what was the saddest event in the book, and what was an event that made them angry. Encourage students to share their interviews.

7. Discuss with the students why slaves had to escape by way of the Underground Railroad. Ask the students how the slaves who ran the Underground Railroad were resisting slavery? What other forms of resistance can they think of in which the slaves participated?

8. Using all of the information the students have read, have the class complete the Newspaper Article on page 35. The students need only to make up information that they believe would be true according to what they have learned about slaves from the book.

Slavery Journals

Materials:

- construction paper, one sheet for each student
- lined paper
- glue
- pictures of scenes depicting slavery

Teacher Directions: To create the journals, the students will fold the construction paper and all the white paper in half. The white paper will be slipped inside the construction paper and fastened to form a book or journal. Paste the picture on the cover to complete the slavery journal. As students read *To Be A Slave,* facilitate a discussion regarding the topics that each chapter covers and how the students react. Then have the students write their reactions and feelings to the book in their Slavery Journal. The journal should be written from the student to a former slave. This could be an imaginary person or one found in the book. Reflections should occur daily throughout the reading of the novel. The students will be sharing their feelings on the topic with this slave as if they were writing him or her a letter. The teacher may have daily closure in which the students share what they wrote on a volunteer basis or the teacher may collect the journals daily or weekly and write a reaction to the students' entries. The reaction should be positive and supportive of the students' feelings.

Topic Suggestions:

Chapter 1 – What is it like to be owned? How are the slaves treated?

Chapter 2 – How did the auction block affect the lives of the slaves?

Chapter 3 – Describe the lifestyle of a slave on the plantation

Chapter 4 – Choose one or two slaves from the chapter and describe how they resisted slavery.

Chapter 5 – Describe the different roles the slaves played in the Underground Railroad.

Chapter 6 – What was emancipation and was it good for all slaves?

Chapter 7 – What happened to the slaves after they had their freedom? Were all things equal?

Sample student entry:

Reading—Chapter 2, pages 39–46

Dear Lucy,

I can't believe how you were treated today at the auction. Weren't you crushed when your master sold you and you couldn't even say goodbye to your husband and child? I don't know if I could have been strong enough to live back then. You had to work hard all day and then you weren't even guaranteed the comfort of your family! I wonder if you ever got to see them again. I know that chances are that you didn't, but maybe you did. It's hard to understand that most slaves rejoiced when a child died at a young age. I understand, though, because I wouldn't want my child being sold away from me and forced to work their whole life for nothing. I am sorry for all your suffering, and I just don't understand. . . .

Until tomorrow . . . André

Historical Research

Directions: Research topics related to slavery in order to understand the historical background. Information can be found in any encyclopedia or book that is slavery-related. Choose one of the topics below and write down three things that you do not know about it. Then look up the topic in a research source and record what you learned, your opinion of what you read regarding slavery, and where you found your information. Once you have finished the outline, write a three-paragraph essay using the same format as below. Be sure to have the teacher or a peer edit your essay before you begin your final draft.

Topics:

1. Slavery in Ancient Greece, Rome, Mesopotamia, or Africa
2. The English Slave Trade
3. Conditions on slave ships
4. African Americans fighting in the Civil War
5. The Emancipation Proclamation

Suggested Research Sources:

1. Use any encyclopedia; research under the topic of "Slavery."
2. *Slavery: History: Historians* by Peter Parish (Harper and Row Publishers, 1989)—This study of American slavery gives a concise explanation of American slavery and its impact on slaves and American culture.
3. *Slavery—A World History* by Milton Meltzer (Da Capo Press, 1993)—Milton Meltzer discusses slavery from its origins in prehistoric societies through the peak of the slave trade in the United States Civil War.
4. *Bound for America—The Forced Migration of Africans to the New World* by James Haskins and Kathleen Benson (Lothrop, Lee and Shepard Books, 1999)—This book discusses slavery beginning in the 16th century and the impact it had on Africa, North and South America, and Europe. It contains detailed explanation of slave trade and slave ships.
5. The Web sites listed on page 79 can be used to conduct further research.

Research Outline:

Topic selected _____

1. Three unknown facts: _____
2. What you learned: _____
3. Your opinion of what you learned: _____
4. Sources used to locate information: _____

Vocabulary Scramble

Directions: Using the Historical Background on page 5 and the definition, unscramble the vocabulary word, and write it on the line.

1. (eminmu) _____ protected from a disease or infection; as by inoculation

2. (lasve) _____ a person who is property of another

3. (lbesiscpeut) _____ subject to an influence; as in a cold

4. (arblo) _____ productive activity

5. (iedasess) _____ illnesses

6. (ulrcatvei) _____ profitable; moneymaking

7. (tacpuder) _____ taken by force or seized

8. (ctsaerhmn) _____ persons whose business is buying and selling goods for profit

9. (eognattadei) _____ dealt or bargained with another or others

10. (ncoidtoni) _____ particular state or situation of a person or thing—state of health

11. (pftrio) _____ the monetary surplus after all expenses of a business transaction or venture have been met

12. (fcoimeentnn) _____ enclosed; kept in bounds, shut up as in prison

13. (tlio) _____ exhausting labor or effort

14. (grdueryd) _____ performing menial, dull, or hard work

15. (eishoud) _____ horrible or frightful to the senses

16. (sldosteae) _____ feeling of being friendless or hopeless; forlorn

17. (urcluet) _____ the ways of living developed by a human group and transmitted to succeeding generations

28. (olabshi) _____ to do away with; put an end to

29. (mpraatn) _____ prevailing or unchecked; widespread

20. (cipenmoainta) _____ freedom of a slave from bondage

20. (icvryto) _____ success against any opponent, opposition, or difficulty

22. (rpnoicoltaam) _____ an official or formal announcement

23. (ueltiyqa) _____ to be or become equal

The Auction Block Discussion

Work in small groups to discuss the following questions or statements. Use the book, *To Be A Slave*, and other resource materials to help with your discussion. After you have discussed each question, be sure each group member writes his or her own answers on a separate sheet of paper.

Questions and Statements for Small Group Discussion:

1. Why did slave owners generally sell their slaves?

2. Virginia was known as a slave-breeding state. What was the believed advantage of breeding slaves?

3. Describe some of the emotions that slaves experienced when they were sold and separated from their families at auctions.

4. Describe the job of a slave trader.

5. Why was there a rush by some slave owners to sell their slaves when Abraham Lincoln was elected President in 1860? How did the slave trader make the slaves look healthier and easier to sell?

6. What happened to the slaves once they were sold to a trader? What was a slave coffle and a slave jail?

7. Describe two sorrowful situations that occurred at the auction block and describe one surprisingly joyful situation.

8. What different modes of transportation did a slave trader use to transport slaves to their new "homes"?

9. Why was it more common to see slave coffles between the months of October and May?

10. What condition do you think the slaves were in once they reached their destination?

11. What did the slaves do as they marched along the roads?

12. If you were a slave trader, how would you justify or explain your job to those who were against slavery?

13. How do you think other slaves felt when they saw the slave trader and his coffle coming?

Describe the Plantation

Most slaves grew up or at least worked and lived on a plantation. While reading Chapter 3, "The Plantation," one should note the varying descriptions of the plantation, depending on the wealth of a master, the location, and slave quarters. Quotes taken from *To Be A Slave* that describe the plantations are found below. Choose one descriptive sentence that appeals to your senses. Use your knowledge of slavery thus far and your imagination to write a descriptive paragraph of a plantation and its activities based on the sentence chosen.

1. "It was a large white mansion, with fluted columns and a broad porch; massive trees spread their limbs over a circular driveway which led up to the house."

2. "My master's house was made of brick . . . and contained two large parlors and a spacious hall or entry on the ground floor."

3. "There was a spacious garden behind the house, containing, I believe, about five acres, well-cultivated and handsomely laid out."

4. "We lodged in log huts and on the bare ground."

5. "Their quarters were comfortable brick dwellings with real floors, doors that shut tight, and windows with glass panes."

Description:_____

_____

_____

_____

_____

_____

_____

_____

_____

_____

_____

_____

Resistance to Slavery

True or False

Directions: Complete the quiz below. On the line beside the statement, write whether that statement is True or False. On the back of the paper, explain why the ones marked false are false and rewrite the false statements to make them true.

1. _____ Slave owners used religion to control the minds of the slaves.

2. _____ Slaves were able to keep the name of their fathers.

3. _____ Slaves created their own religion, based on the white Southerner's Christianity.

4. _____ According to the religion of the slaves, the slaves believed that they would receive an award for their suffering after they died.

5. _____ Slave owners and slaves both believed in the same idea of heaven.

6. _____ Religion was used as a form of resistance for the slaves.

7. _____ Slave owners controlled the slaves with religion and the whip.

8. _____ The slave owners controlled the minds of the slaves with the idea of natural superiority of the white man and the natural inferiority of the black man.

9. _____ African languages are similar to English, and therefore, it was easy for the slaves to learn English.

10. _____ Thomas Jefferson wrote an essay describing the equality of the whites and blacks.

11. _____ Slaves who were African natives did not believe in the inferiority of blacks that the white man claimed because they had a former life to dispute the idea of inferiority.

12. _____ "Uncle Toms" were slaves who resented the white master and rebelled against slavery.

13. _____ The master often turned the house servants against the field servants and would reward the betrayal of a fellow slave.

14. _____ Many slaves attempted to gain favor with their master in order provide for their families with rewards of food or money.

15. _____ Josh Henson was a typical slave who did not care about his master's approval.

14

The Slaves' Social Life

Slaves had very few activities that they were able to enjoy. Using the list the class generated on the board, choose three of the activities that slaves may have been able to enjoy and rank them in the order that you would enjoy most: first, second, and third. Then answer the questions that follow.

1. The activity I would enjoy . . .

   first is _____

   second is_____

   third is _____

2. Why did you choose your "first choice" activity? What would make it so enjoyable?

   _____

   _____

   _____

   _____

3. Do you believe that slaves were allowed the opportunity to socialize very often? Why or why not?

   _____

   _____

   _____

   _____

4. What did their masters do to prevent the slaves from meeting together at night?

   _____

   _____

   _____

   _____

Anti-Slavery Speech

Directions: Using the speech format below, choose one of the two topics and write a persuasive speech.

Elements of a Speech

Introduction: A good introduction sets the direction of your speech. It needs to get the attention of your audience, introduce your topic, state your central idea or purpose, briefly identify the main points, and make your audience anxious to hear what you have to say about that topic. Some attention getting ideas are: telling your audience an amazing fact; telling a funny story; giving a short demonstration or using a visual aid; asking a series of questions or giving a short history of the topic; and giving a strong statement about why the topic is important to you and your audience.

Body: The body of a speech carries the main arguments or points of the topic. Organization of the body is very important. You can organize in order of importance, least to greatest or greatest to least. You can organize in the order of which events take place. Another way to organize is in a problem/solution format in which you describe the problem and then present a solution to solve it.

Conclusion: The conclusion helps your audience understand what they have heard, why it's important, and what they should do about it. You may want to restate your main idea and use an attention-getting device like in the introduction.

Topic #1 — Anti-Slavery Speech

Toward the end of the Civil War, many slaves were not sure if their freedom would be won. Pretend you are a slave and write a persuasive speech that justifies the freedom of the slaves.

Introduction: Use background information of slavery or your background as a slave.

Body: Tell about slavery as you know it. Describe the living conditions of slaves, the working conditions of slaves, their deaths, and their lack of social freedoms. Describe anything of the slaves' situation that would persuade freedom.

Conclusion: Discuss the benefits of freedom and what slaves will be able to contribute to society as free individuals.

Topic #2 — Pro-Slavery Speech

Many Southerners and slave owners were in favor of the institution of slavery. The idea that slavery might be abolished was very frightening to the Southerners. Write a speech that is persuasive in justifying slavery.

Introduction: Use background information from the perspective of master who owns slaves.

Body: State the advantages of slavery to the economy of the South. List the conditions that slaves live under on your plantation. Describe your religion and that, according to it, slaves are in their appropriate place in society.

Conclusion: Discuss the benefits that the slaves and the white southern economy will experience because of slavery.

Letters from a Slave Girl—
The Story of Harriet Jacobs

by Mary E. Lyons

Summary

Harriet Jacobs was born into slavery. She is fortunate to be surrounded by her grandmother, brother, and other family members. However, when her mistress dies, she is left at the mercy of the mistress' will. She is sent to live with a terrible family. This horrible experience may give her the strength to escape to the North. She suffers many trials before her chance comes and with the strength she is blessed with, she may survive. Based on the true story of Harriet Ann Jacobs, her letters reveal the horrible ordeals that African-Americans had to endure under slavery.

The outline below is a suggested plan for using the various activities that are presented in this unit. You should adopt these to fit your own classroom situation.

Sample Plan

Lesson 1

❏ Send home parent letter on page 20.

❏ Go over vocabulary and the dedication ("Setting the Stage," page 18, activity 1).

❏ Read Part I, the first section on "Mama."

❏ Discuss "Setting the Stage," page 18, activity 3.

❏ Discuss the foods that Harriet ate and made.

❏ As a class, complete "Making Crackers" (page 21).

❏ Discuss Harriet's slavery situation:

— alone without her mother, hopeful for freedom

— given to Dr. Norcom family

— living in a house with "cold folk"

— worrying about her brother

Lesson 2

❏ Read Section I, "Papa."

❏ Discuss Harriet's letters to her father ("Enjoying the Book", page 18, activity 1)

❏ Read Section I, second section on "Mama."

❏ Read Section I, "R."

❏ Assign "Comprehension Questions" (page 22).

❏ Do "Character Traits" (page 23).

❏ Do "Enjoying the Book," page 18, activity 4.

❏ Complete "Your Life" (page 24).

Lesson 3

❏ Read Part II.

❏ Discuss all that Harriet does for her freedom:

— deals with Dr. Norcom's inappropriate behavior

— asks Samuel for help

— runs away at night

— hides out at Gran's and in the swamps

❏ Assign "The Underground Railroad" (page 36–39).

❏ Discuss similes and metaphors (page 25).

Lesson 4

❏ Continue reading Part III.

❏ Discuss Harriet's family tree. ("Extending the Book," page 19, activity 2)

❏ Assign "Interview for a Family Tree" (page 26).

❏ Assign "Autobiography" (page 27).

❏ Do "Extending the Book," page 19, activity 4.

❏ Do "Extending the Book," page 19, activity 5.

Overview of Activities

Setting the Stage

1. Before reading the book, go over the vocabulary toward the end of the book in the section labeled "Nineteenth Century Vocabulary." Also read the dedication with the class. Ask the students: Why do you think this book is dedicated to women who seek freedom from oppression? From the little you know about Harriet Jacobs, what oppression do you think she was under?

2. Complete the letter to parents on page 20, and send it home before the class begins reading the book.

3. Read Part I, the first section on "Mama." Discuss why the students think Harriet is writing to her mother. Is she writing to her for her own comfort? Why does Harriet need her mother at this time? Is Harriet writing about things that she could only discuss with her mother?

4. As a class activity, complete "Making Crackers" on page 21.

Enjoying the Book

1. Read Part I, "Papa," and discuss why Harriet is writing to her father. Does she miss him? What is her father's personality like? What does she talk to her father about? Why is he a comfort to her?

2. Read Part I, the sections on "Mama" and "R," and assign "Comprehension Questions" on page 22 to assess the comprehension of the book thus far.

3. Discuss Harriet's life in hiding (For example: the weather, insects, watching her children grow up not knowing her, and not being able to move for hours). Ask the students if they think all of that is worth freedom.

4. Discuss all the different characters in the book and create a chart on the board to identify who they are and what their connection is to Harriet.

5. The characters in Harriet's life have many different personalities. Personalities impact the way people live their lives and the decisions one makes. Discuss personality traits and have the students complete "Character Traits" on page 23.

6. Harriet writes about her life and all of her experiences, both good and bad. Tell the students to explore their lives by completing page 24.

18

Overview of Activities *(cont.)*

Extending the Book

1. Harriet uses many similes and metaphors to make her writing more descriptive. Discuss the uses of similes and metaphors, and have the students complete the activity on page 25.

2. At the end of the book there is a diagram of Harriet's family tree. Give the students time to look this over, and then assign "Interview for a Family Tree" on page 26.

3. Through her letters, Harriet writes the story of her life, or her autobiography. Discuss different autobiographies the students may have read. Ask them what they would put in their own autobiography and assign page 27.

4. Allow the students time to look at the pictures of Harriet and the places she lived at the end of the book. Discuss how seeing the pictures made the story more real and brought Harriet to life.

5. Many other people in history have been oppressed and forced into hiding because of the circumstances in society. Another young woman who was forced into hiding in a different era was Anne Frank. Encourage the students to check out a book on Anne Frank and discuss the similarities in their years of hiding.

Parent Letter

_____
      (Date)

Dear Parents,

As a part of our Slavery Thematic Unit, we will be reading *Letters from a Slave Girl—The Story of Harriet Jacobs* by Mary E. Lyons. This book is about Harriet Jacobs, a slave who endured much hardship to gain her freedom. The story is very powerful and very realistic as to what actually occurred in the time of slavery. Your child may have questions that he/she may discuss with you. If you have any concerns or would like more information about the book, please contact me.

In the book, Harriet learns how to make crackers from scratch. As a class project we are going to make the crackers from Harriet's recipe and a traditional African American recipe for cornbread. There are some supplies that we will need, and I am asking for donations. Below is list of the necessary supplies.

- 5 lbs (2.3 kg) flour
- 5 lbs (2.3 kg) sugar
- 1 container of salt
- 4 sticks (1 lb/450 g) butter
- 1 quart (960 mL) milk

- 1 lb (450 g) cornmeal
- 1 container baking powder
- 1 quart (960 mL) buttermilk
- ½ dozen eggs
- 1 pint (1.1 L) vegetable oil

If you can donate any supplies, please check the item and write in the quantity. Please return the bottom section of this letter as soon as possible and I will contact you regarding the date that the ingredients should be brought to school. Thanks again for your support.

Sincerely,

_____
      (Teacher)

Yes, I will bring in the following (please write in the quantity):

_____ flour	_____ butter	_____ baking powder
_____ sugar	_____ milk	_____ eggs
_____ salt	_____ cornmeal	_____ oil

Name _____

Phone number at home _____

Phone number at work _____

Making Crackers

Slaves, who worked in the "big house" or the home of the master, often were in charge of cooking, cleaning, and looking after the children. "Soul Food" was derived from slave cooking. Meals were cooked over open fires or barbecued in open pits because there were few stoves, and the slaves certainly didn't use them unless they were cooking for their masters.

You learned in Part I that Harriet is a house slave. She learned how to make crackers and included the recipe in her letter. Follow Harriet's recipe to make your own crackers.

Ingredients:

- 1 lb (450 g) flour
- 1 cup (240 mL) sugar
- 4 good pinches of salt
- ½ stick (¼ c/60 mL) of butter
- ½ cup (120mL) milk

Utensils:

fork, spoon, bowl, measuring cup, rolling pin, cookie cutter (or glass), and a baking sheet

Directions:

Mix all the dry ingredients together. Add butter and mix thoroughly. Slowly add the milk until well mixed. Roll out the dough until flat and thin. Cut the crackers using a cookie cutter or a glass turned upside down. Bake at 350°F (180°C) just until golden brown.

Cornbread

Slaves were often forced to eat the scraps that their masters didn't want. They often created wonderful dishes out of these scraps. Some of these foods are bread pudding, greens, sweet potato pie, and cornbread. Follow the recipe below and make some cornbread like the slaves used to eat.

Ingredients:

- 1½ cups (360 mL) cornmeal
- ¾ cup (180 mL) flour
- 2½ teaspoons (12.5 mL) baking powder
- ½ teaspoon (2.5 mL) salt
- 1¼ cups (300 mL) buttermilk
- 2 eggs
- 2 tablespoons (30 mL) oil

Utensils:

9-inch pan greased, bowl, spoon or fork

Directions:

Mix all ingredients in a bowl. Pour mixture into pan and bake at 425°F (220°C) for 18 minutes.

Enrichment:

- Research other foods that slaves ate or made.

- Make a food from the period of slavery with your family and bring samples to the class.

Comprehension Questions

Directions: Answer the following questions. Make sure your answer is written in a complete sentence.

1. What happened to Harriet's father? How did she feel about it?

   _____

2. What is working from "can to can't" according to Gran?

   _____

3. What did Harriet think of the fact that the party of gentlemen had dinner on the ice?

   _____

4. Why was Harriet punished for the first time? What happened because of her punishment?

   _____

5. What was the story of two runaway slaves that Harriet thought was sweet?

   _____

6. How does Harriet's brother, John, feel about slavery? What did he do that demonstrated his feelings?

   _____

7. With what did Harriet re-stuff the mattresses?

   _____

8. What promise did Miss Elizabeth Horniblow keep in her will?

   _____

9. What happened at the slave auction?

   _____

10. Who did Harriet meet at the dance? How did she feel about this meeting?

    _____

11. What wonderful thing did Miss Hannah do for Gran? Why do you think she did this?

    _____

12. How long was Gran a slave?

    _____

13. When "R" came back from working in Washington County, what did he have and why?

    _____

14. Who was going to protect Harriet from Doctor Norcom?

    _____

15. What is the doctor's plan to get Harriet alone with him? Do you think his plan will work? Why or why not?

    _____

Character Traits

The characters in *Letters from a Slave Girl* have very different personalities. Using Harriet's descriptions and the adjectives below, place the adjectives that describe each character on the line beside their name. You may use the adjectives more than once. Finally, complete the paragraph that follows.

Adjectives

strong-willed	rude	scared	wise
kindhearted	protective	controlling	discriminatory
angry	caring	faithful	ignorant
hurtful	vengeful	intelligent	righteous
happy	mean	harsh	gullible
bitter	sweet	unfair	concerned

Harriet: _____

_____

John: _____

_____

Gran: _____

_____

Doctor Norcom: _____

_____

Mrs. Norcom: _____

_____

Hannah (Miss Elizabeth Horniblow's sister):_____

_____

Samuel Sawyer: _____

_____

Paragraph: Compare and contrast the way Harriet and Gran deal with their situations in slavery. Keep in mind their different personalities and the varying traits you listed for them above. Is one more accepting of slavery than the other? Do they both oppose slavery but in different ways? Explain.

_____

_____

_____

_____

_____

_____

Your Life

Just as Harriet records the ups and downs of her life in letters, write down ten significant events that have happened to you and the year that they occurred. Be sure that there are both positive and negative events. For example: Your birth is a positive event, while falling off your bike and breaking your arm is a negative event.

Next, take a string or piece of yarn and tie ten separate knots in the yarn. Be sure that the knots representing the events are tied in order and that you leave enough space between each knot to reflect how far apart each event took place in years. For instance, if two events occurred two months apart, then the knots will be close together. If, however, the events occurred ten years apart, the knots will be further apart.

After you have made your knots, think of a shape or design that represents you, your experiences, or your likes or dislikes. On a sheet of paper, create the design with your string and glue it in place. Then write next to each knot, the year and what event it represents. You have now created a representation of your life.

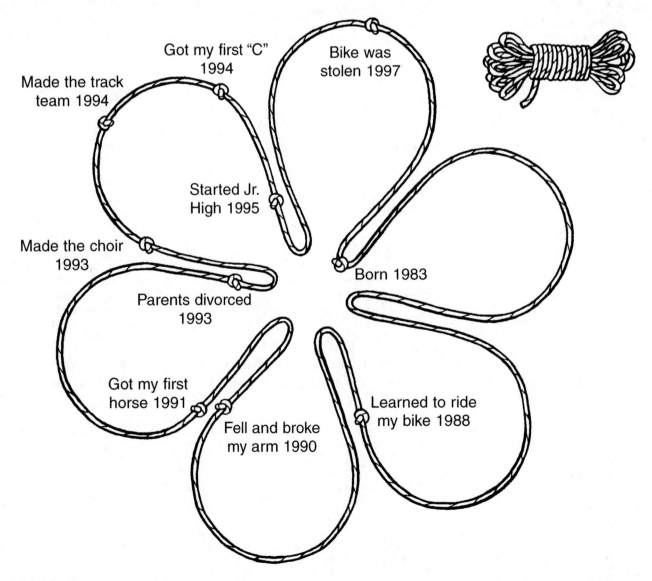

Similes and Metaphors

A **simile** is a figure of speech in which one thing is likened to a dissimilar thing using like or as.
Example: My mind is like a rat running in circles.

A **metaphor** is a figure of speech in which one thing is likened to a dissimilar thing by being spoken of as if it were that other thing. *Example:* My mind is a rat running around in circles.

Throughout Harriet's letters she uses similes and metaphors to describe her experiences and how she is feeling. Read the similes and metaphors taken from Harriet's letters. On the line below them, first write whether it is a simile or a metaphor, and then try to explain what you think the expression means.

1. "Time is a whisper I can't hear."

   _____

   _____

2. "The Norcoms, they are two limbs from the same tree."

   _____

   _____

3. "When they help me down the first time, I sway like a sapling in the wind, then my ankles give way."

   _____

4. "But slavery must be like that claret he likes to drink. It's just too good to give up."

   _____

   _____

5. "Each time the clouds hang heavy and dark, and like a monster, the hurricane springs right at us from the sea."

   _____

   _____

6. "So my babies are trapped between two monsters, like rabbits cornered by hound dogs."

   _____

   _____

7. "John, seems like all these years I been a foolish puppy."

   _____

   _____

8. "They only shadows to me now, like when nighttime crowds the trees and pushed them out of sight."

   _____

   _____

9. "Peter is just coming to see me, grinning like a man in the moon."

   _____

   _____

10. "Time. It creeps and pokes along like a mule all these years."

    _____

    _____

Interview for a Family Tree

At the end of *Letters from a Slave Girl,* there is a diagram of Harriet's family tree. Creating a family tree is an excellent way to discover your "roots"—the people who came before you in your family. You can also discover where your family is from and perhaps find some interesting facts or stories about family members. Feel free to ask parents, brothers, sisters, or any other relative to help you complete the project. Fill in the interview questions below after speaking with members of your family. If you cannot find information about some family members, leave the line blank. Then complete a family tree for your own family on a separate piece of paper.

My Family:

1. What are the names of your grandparents, and when were they born?

    _____

    _____

2. When were your grandparents married?

    _____

    _____

3. What are the names of your grandparent's children (including your parents)? List them in the order they were born.

    _____

    _____

    _____

4. List the names of your brothers and sisters and their ages, in order.

    _____

    _____

5. Which family member(s) was the most difficult to find any information about? Why?

    _____

    _____

6. Did you learn anything interesting about a particular family member? If so, what?

    _____

    _____

7. Where is your family from originally?

    _____

    _____

8. Did you learn about any family member that you hadn't known about?

    _____

    _____

9. What area of your family's history would you like to know more about?

    _____

    _____

Autobiography

Many authors have written biographies or stories of the lives of slaves. Slaves had fascinating experiences that many people today cannot comprehend. Biographies enable people to understand the thoughts and experiences of others. Some slaves wrote their own autobiographies or the story of their own lives. Autobiographies tend to be more accurate because they are written from the perspective of the person who actually lived the life.

Using the brainstorming map below, fill in the events of your life and write an autobiography. Your autobiography will not be as long or as detailed as the biography of Harriet Jacobs or other biographies you may have read. Your autobiography should be a maximum of two pages but no less than one full page. You have not lived as long as Harriet and you most likely have not yet experienced as many things as she did. Remember to brainstorm first, write the rough draft, edit your work (with a peer or the teacher), and then write the final draft.

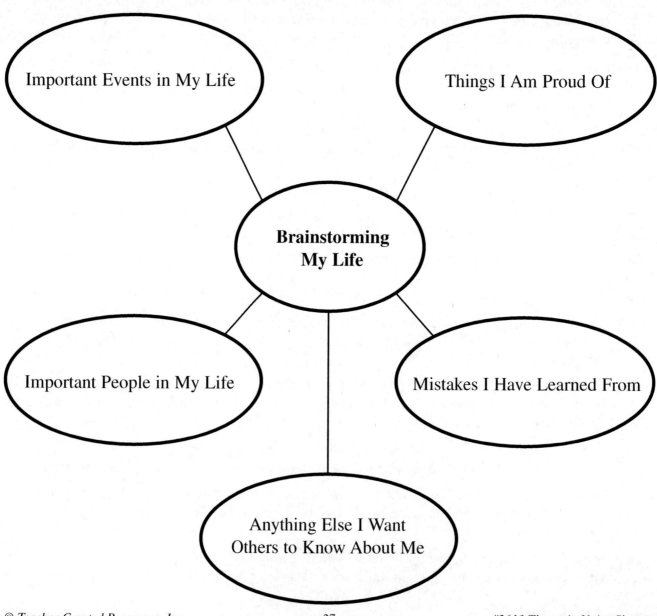

Further Reading Selections

Enjoy some of these other works about slavery.

Ayers, Katherine. *North by Night: A Story of the Underground Railroad.* (Delacorte Press, 1998).
Presents the journal of a sixteen-year-old girl whose family operates a stop on the Underground Railroad.

Chbosky, Stacy. *Who Owns the Sun?* (Landmark Editions, Inc., 1988).
An emotion packed story of a young slave who touches the human spirit.

Coleman, Evelyn. *To Be A Drum.* (Albert Whitman & Co., 1998).
Daddy Wes tells how Africans were brought to America as slaves.

Duey, Kathleen. *Evie Peach, St. Louis, 1857.* (Aladdin Paperbacks, 1997).
Emancipated by their owner's will, a family struggles to make a home for themselves in the pre-Civil War South.

Hathorn, Elizabeth. *Sky Sash So Blue.* (Simon & Schuster Books for Young Readers, 1998).
The special sky blue sash that a young slave girl gives her older sister becomes a tie that bonds the family together.

Houston, Gloria. *Bright Freedom's Song: A Story of the Underground Railroad.* (Harcourt Brace, 1998).
Before the Civil War, Bright discovers that her parents are providing a safe house for the Underground Railroad.

Nardo, Don. *Braving the New World 1619–1784.* (Chelsea House Publishers, 1947).
This book offers a view of African slave trade, the birth of African-American culture, and portraits of famous black Americans.

Polacco, Patricia. *Pink and Say.* (Scholastic, Inc., 1994).
A written memory of Pinkus Aylee, an African American who fought in the Civil War and befriended a wounded soldier who happened to be white.

Rappaport, Doreen. *Escape from Slavery: Five Journeys to Freedom.* (Harper Collins Publishers, 1991).
The stories of five African Americans who managed to find freedom before the American Civil War.

Reeder, Carolyn. *Across the Lines.* (Atheneum Books for Young Readers, 1997).
A white plantation owner's son and his black house servant and friend, witness the siege of Petersburg during the Civil War.

Wallin, Luke. *The Slavery Ghosts.* (Bradbury Press, 1983).
This book is about an old haunted mansion whose ghosts were slaves who dug underground tunnels there in the 1850s. Two children have to put the ghosts to rest.

Washington, Margaret. *Narrative of Sojourner Truth.* (Vintage Books, 1993).
A partial autobiography of a woman who's story explores the unknown world of Northern slavery.

Whitmore, Arvella. *Trapped Between the Lash and the Gun; a Boy's Journey.* (Dial Books, 1999).
A young, troubled boy is suddenly transported through time and becomes a slave on the plantation of his ancestors.

Winter, Jeanette. *Follow the Drinking Gourd.* (Alfred P. Knopf Dragonfly Books, 1988).
A picture book about the Underground Railroad and the ways the slaves navigated to the North.

Br'er Rabbit Builds a Home

Folk stories are one way people pass down legends and beliefs from their culture to the younger generations. Slaves were told many folk stories that passed the time, were a source of entertainment, and taught young African-American children lessons on how to deal with the "white man's world." Slaves often used a trickster in their stories like Br'er Rabbit to either laugh at or to teach a lesson. Many believe that African Americans likened the trickster to themselves in their weakened position of slavery. Although this character seems weaker, he often seems to come out victorious and outsmart those who seem to be brighter. Most of the tricks these characters take on are for the sheer challenge of solving the problem. The trickster will go from one self-created problem to the next. Although many people who told these stories would refer to them as entertainment, lies, and nonsense, be assured that there was a larger truth hidden within them. Read the following African-American folk story, and then complete the activities that follow.

Br'er Rabbit Builds a Home
by Jackie Torrence

All the creatures in the big wood—Br'er Possum, Br'er Coon, Br'er Wolf, and Br'er Rabbit—decided they should work together and build a house.

They each took different jobs. Br'er Rabbit insisted that he'd have to do something on the ground because he couldn't climb ladders, which made him dizzy in the head. And he couldn't work outside because the sun made him shiver. So he got himself a ruler and stuck a pencil behind his ear and started measuring and marking, marking and measuring. He was in and out, all around, so busy that the other creatures really thought he was putting down a whole passel of work. Yet all the while he was just marking time, doing absolutely nothing.

The critters that was workin', was workin'. They built a fine house, the likes of which nobody in those parts had ever seen. Why, if the truth be known, it was a splendid house: plenty of upstairs rooms, plenty of downstairs rooms, a whole heap of chimneys, fireplaces, and all sorts of other wonderful things.

After the house was finished, each critter picked a room. Old Br'er Rabbit picked one of the upstairs rooms and proceeded to furnish it. While all the other critters were busy finishing their rooms, Br'er Rabbit was slipping three things into his room: a shotgun, a big black cannon, and a big tin tub of water.

When everything was all finished in the house, they cooked a big supper to celebrate. Then everyone took a seat in the parlor.

Br'er Rabbit sat for a while, and then he yawned and stretched and excused himself for bed. The other creatures stayed on and laughed and talked and had a good time in their new parlor.

While they were talking and laughing, Br'er Rabbit yelled from his room, "When a big fella like me wants to sit down, whereabouts do you think he ought to sit?"

All the other critters just laughed and said, "When a big feller like you can't sit in a chair, he better sit on the floor."

Br'er Rabbit Builds a Home *(cont.)*

"Watch out down there, 'cause I'm fixin' to sit right now," yelled Br'er Rabbit. He pulled the trigger of the shotgun. Ka-boom!

Well, all the critters looked at each other and wondered, what in the world was that? But everything was quiet then and nobody said anything for a long time.

After a while the critters forgot the noise and started talking and laughing again. Then Br'er Rabbit stuck his head out the door again and said, "When a big fella like me wants to sneeze, whereabouts can he sneeze?"

The other creatures hollered up the stairs, "When a big feller like you can't hold a sneeze, he can sneeze where he pleases."

Watch out down there, 'cause I'm gonna sneeze right here," said Br'er Rabbit. And he lit the fuse on the cannon. Ka-boom!

Well, the sound of the cannon knocked the critters out of their chairs. The blast shook in the windows, the dishes rattled in the cupboard, and Br'er Bear hit the floor, right on his bottom.

"Lordsey be," said Br'er Bear, "I think Br'er Rabbit has a powerful bad cold. I think I'm gonna step outside for a breath of fresh air."

All the critters settled down again and were talking among themselves when Br'er Rabbit yelled out another time, "When a big feller like me wants to take a chew of tobacco, whereabouts is he supposed to spit?"

The other critters hollered back to Br'er Rabbit, mad as they could be, "If you be a big man or a little man, spit where you please."

"Look out down there!" yelled Br'er Rabbit, "I'm gonna spit!" About that time he turned over the tub of water and it came rolling down the steps. Ker-splash!

Well, every one of the critters heard it coming at the same time. They all took off in different directions. Some jumped out of the windows, some bolted through the doors, everyone went in a different direction, but they all cleared out of the house.

Old Br'er Rabbit locked the doors, closed the windows, went to bed, and slept like he owned the world. And that's how Br'er Rabbit built a home.

Reprinted with the permission of Simon & Schuster from *JUMP UP AND SAY HI* by Linda Goss and Clay Goss. Copyright © 1995 by Linda and Clay Goss.

Activity:

On a separate sheet of paper, re-write the ending to the Br'er Rabbit story. Try to be creative and make an original ending to this folk story. Start the new ending right after all the creatures settle into the house and have the celebration dinner. Think of how Br'er Rabbit could have gotten the house in different ways. Have fun!

30

Famous Quotations

Directions: Following are quotes taken from African Americans who either experienced or observed slavery. On the lines following each quotation, try to paraphrase—tell in your own words—what you think that person meant, how they felt about slavery, and what they were saying about their situation or slavery in general.

1. "There is a debt to the Negro people which America can never repay. At least then, they must make amends."—Sojourner Truth

   _____

   _____

   _____

2. "With freedom they suddenly found themselves in the position where they had to supply their own needs. All were willing and able to do so, but to do so they required land of their own and farm equipment to get started. To be really free, it was necessary that they not have to go to those who had formerly held them as slaves and ask for jobs."—Julius Lester

   _____

   _____

   _____

3. "I started with this idea in my head, 'There's two things I've got a right to, death or liberty.'"
   —Harriet Tubman

   _____

   _____

   _____

4. "I would fight for my liberty so long as my strength lasted, and if the time came for me to go, the Lord would let them take me."—Harriet Tubman

   _____

   _____

   _____

5. "The bright joyous dreams of freedom to the slave faded—were sadly altered, in the presence of that stern, practical mother, reality."—Elizabeth Keckly.

   _____

   _____

   _____

6. "Its aim was to brainwash the slave, to destroy his mind and replace it with the mind of the master. In that way the slave would enslave himself and there would be no need to police him. A slave would have no sense of himself that was separate from the self the master wanted him to have."—Julius Lester

   _____

   _____

   _____

Famous Quotations *(cont.)*

7. "Sing! I say they did sing. Sing about the cooking and about the milking and sing in the field."
—Hannah Hancock

_____

_____

_____

8. "Freedom. One day they awakened by the sound of the overseer's horn. The next day they were
not. One morning they had gone to the fields and before the sun set, they had left their hoes, their
plows, their cotton sacks lying in the furrows."—Julius Lester

_____

_____

_____

9. "Over the hills they would come in lines reaching as far as you could see. They walked in double
lines chained together in twos. The slavers walked them here to the railroad and shipped them in
coal cars to the cotton country."—Lorenzo Ivy

_____

_____

_____

10. "A Negro has got no name. . . . If you belong to Mr. Jones and he sell you to Mr. Johnson,
consequently you go by the name of your owner. . . . We are wearing the name of our master. I
was first a Hale; then my father was sold and then I was named Reed."—Anonymous

_____

_____

_____

11. "Then she yelled, 'I'm free! Yes, I'm free! Ain't gonna work for you no more. You can't put me
in your pocket now!' Granma say Missus Thacker started boo—hooing. . . . She knew it was true
then."—Betty Jones

_____

_____

_____

The Ballad of the Underground Railroad

Read the following poem. Complete the interpretation section following the poem and then write your own poem about any aspect of slavery you wish. The poem does not have to rhyme. It must be based on facts and real emotions that you have read about. Be creative and allow the voices of the former slaves to speak through your poetry.

The Ballad of the Underground Railroad

Tonight we ride the underground train.
It runs on tracks that are covered with pain.
The whole of Humanity makes up the crew
And Liberty's the engineer to carry us through.
The North Star will lead us,
And Freedom will greet us
When we reach the end of the line.
The Underground Train,
Strange as it seems,
Carried many passengers
And never was seen.
It wasn't made of wood,
It wasn't made of steel;
A man-made train that
Ran without wheels
The train was known,
By many a name.
But the greatest of all
Was "The Freedom Train."
The Quakers, the Indians
Gentiles and Jews,
Were some of the people
Who made up the crews.
Free Blacks and Christians
And Atheists, too,
Were the rest of the people
Who made up the crews.
Conductors and agents
Led the way at night,
Guiding the train
By the North Star Light.
The passengers were
The fugitive slaves
Running from slavery

And its evil ways
Running from the whip
And the overseer,
From the slave block
And the Auctioneer.
They didn't want their masters
To catch them again,
So the men dressed as women
And the women as men
They hid in churches,
Cellars and barns,
Waiting to hear the Train's alarm.
Sleeping by day,
And traveling by night,
Was the best way they knew
To keep out of sight.
They waded in the waters
To hide their scent,
And fool those bloodhounds
The slave masters sent.
They spoke in riddles
And sang in codes,
To understand the message,
You had to be told.
Those who knew the secret
Never did tell
The sacred message
Of the "Freedom Train's" bell.
Riding this train
Broke the laws of the land,
But the laws of God
Are higher than man's.

by Charles L. Blockson

The Ballad of the Underground Railroad *(cont.)*

Interpretation:

What do you think the poet meant by "the whole of Humanity makes up the crew"?

_____

_____

_____

Where was the end of the line for the Underground Railroad?

_____

_____

_____

If, according to the poet, it wasn't a real train, of what was the Underground Railroad made?

_____

_____

_____

Why was it known as "The Freedom Train"?

_____

_____

_____

Why do you think the poet listed all the different types of people who helped with the Railroad? What was he showing?

_____

_____

_____

What do you think the poet meant by "broke the laws of the land"?

_____

_____

_____

What do you think are laws of God? Why do you think the poet thinks these are superior to the laws of the land?

_____

_____

_____

Newspaper Article

You have learned a lot about slavery from reading *To Be A Slave* and *Letters from a Slave Girl* as well as from other research you have completed. Use this information as well as your imagination to complete the sentence starters below.

Pretend you are an escaped slave living in the North and you are writing a newspaper article about your life and experiences. Try to make the article interesting but true to the life of a slave. You will be graded on how realistic your story is according to all that you have learned about slaves and slavery. Be sure to write the concluding sentence on your own.

Escaped Slave Tells All

It all began when _____

_____ . I was only _____ years old when the

worst thing happened to me. I remember it very clearly: _____

_____

_____ . My master often _____

_____ . It was my job

to_____ . That's when I decided _____

_____ . It

was difficult when I had to _____ . My

life changed when_____

_____ . My struggle

wasn't through; I_____

_____ . Then I worked

as a _____ . That's where I met _____ .

We decided that together we would _____ .

It was challenging at first, but _____ .

Then I decided that I wanted to_____

_____ . I helped other slaves by_____

_____ . I eventually grew older and I _____

_____ . I couldn't help anymore because _____

_____ my life because _____

_____ . Without slavery I would never have known

_____ . I am a better person

today because _____ . I

am satisfied with _____

The Underground Railroad

Directions: Read the following passage about Harriet Tubman and the Underground Railroad. Then answer the questions at the end of the passage and do the math activity on page 63.

Harriet Tubman

Harriet Tubman grew up on a Maryland plantation. Even as a young slave, she was known for her independent spirit. Although this often resulted in Harriet receiving many beatings and lashes, her spirit was never broken. She would not act overly polite to find favor in the eyes of her master and receive an easier job as a house slave. In Harriet's eyes, the fields were the place to be. She enjoyed working in the fresh air and sunshine.

Harriet was never content with slavery, as she seldom smiled. She would risk anything to help slaves escape the shackles of slavery. Harriet's desire to be free increased dramatically when she learned slavery was abolished in the North. Soon thereafter, Harriet became a member of the Underground Railroad. The Underground Railroad was a system that helped slaves escape to freedom. She repeatedly returned to her former home state of Maryland to "conduct" or lead slaves to freedom in the North. The job of a "conductor" was very dangerous. Harriet, however, was never caught and never lost a "passenger" on the Underground Railroad. In all, she guided over 300 slaves to freedom.

Even though she was free, she didn't forget her family or other slaves in the South. Freedom of slaves to Harriet was her life's mission, she never forgot from where she came and those who were left behind. Time after time, she returned to the South against the warnings of her Northern friends.

To prevent the slave catchers from recognizing her if they saw her, she often disguised herself. Harriet was clever enough to fool even her former master, John Stewart. One day, Harriet created a plan. She would buy two live chickens and attach them to her waist by their feet, leaving them squawking and dangling. This may seem strange, but she had to be especially crafty! What would be the next step of her plan? In the event that she ran into anyone who might recognize her, including Mr. Stewart, Harriet bent over at the waist while she walked, hobbling about as if she were lame. As she hobbled down the dusty path, Mr. Stewart, her old master himself, appeared suddenly in the distance. As per her plan, Harriet let the chickens go. She vigorously tried to catch the fluttering, sputtering chickens in her lame state but was unsuccessful. Mr. Stewart witnessed this pitiful, old Negro woman, appearing lame and sporting a dirty bonnet, attempting to capture the chickens. Rightly so, Mr. Stewart laughed hysterically as went on his way. Harriet's plan was a success! She quickly rounded up some of Mr. Stewart's most valuable slaves, leading them to the free North.

Future trips down South proved to be equally daunting. Harriet, having to avoid main roads and common ways to be careful, had to wade through swamps and marshes, some of which were full of many seen and unseen "creepy crawlies" such as alligators and snakes. All too frequently, did she have to cramp herself into the back of a buggy or wagon, to take on the appearance of the bulky old luggage. Each trip was an education in and of itself, as she gradually learned where slave catchers would be watching and lying in wait. Harriet could not relax or let her guard down, things could go wrong at every turn of a wagon wheel. Accordingly, Harriet assumed responsibility of all aspects of her mission.

The Underground Railroad *(cont.)*

She had to prepare for the expected and the unexpected. How does one prepare for the unexpected? If a baby started crying, she gave it sleeping medicine. If the wagon driver got caught, she led her group of freed slaves on a different route. In the event that dogs would get on their trail, she covered their scents (or left no scents) by re-routing the trip through murky swamp water. Southerners could not understand how Harriet, who still belonged to John Stewart, could steal slaves from right under their noses. Harriet's reputation continued to escalate with the slaves. In fact, slaves called her "Moses," because like Moses, she led her people out of captivity. Like most slaves, Harriet would sing old spirituals while she worked (although she had to sing very quietly to avoid being heard). Ironically, her song of choice was "Go Down, Moses." When slaves would hear that old spiritual, however faintly, they knew the ticket to freedom was a'coming. Slave owners, especially those who had "lost" slaves, were infuriated by the Harriet's elusiveness. Inevitably, the reward for Harriet's capture, dead or alive, rose to $40,000—an unheard of bounty in those days. Ever increasing numbers of slave catchers began to search for her. Posters with her name and description were plentiful. Even as far north as Wilmington, Delaware, slave catchers pursued her with dollar signs in their eyes.

While Harriet had rescued many slaves, she had not rescued her own family, as they would be under heavy observation and surveillance for obvious reasons. Do not think, even for a second, that she forgot about them. They were one of her motivations in freeing other slaves. She longed to be with her family, especially her husband, John Tubman. John Tubman, however, had forgotten her—he had married someone else! This news hit Harriet like a dagger in the heart, leaving her terribly hurt and angered. She would have to persevere. This was not going to cause her to retire to the North and abandon her life's work. Harriet pressed on, allowing herself to forget John Tubman.

Freeing her family became top priority. She began to prepare for her next mission; however, she quickly realized that her major obstacle was money for supplies. In Philadelphia, an opportunity as a scrubwoman emerged and Harriet jumped at the opportunity. During the two or three months she worked, word got to her that her three brothers had been sold. The day after Christmas they were to be shipped out of the family cabin. Upon hearing this news, she harvested her resources and set out for her family's slave quarters. Taking refuge in an abandoned shed, Harriet noticed a small slave boy wandering the plantation. She got his attention and instructed him to give her brothers the message that she was in the shed, and that they needed to meet her there after sunset. Now, Harriet's mother was on that plantation, but she could not let her mother know she was there. Indeed, Harriet's mother would be so overcome with delight and excitement at her daughter's "homecoming," but, she would be grief-stricken at the thought of losing her three sons. Harriet could not risk her mother's excitement, and later, grief, being heard by anyone. "Old Rit," Harriet's mother, was planning a huge Christmas dinner. Harriet faced a very tough decision. Should Harriet let her brothers and their families go to the Christmas dinner or should they flee to the North? She decided that it would be best if they did not attend the dinner. They would prepare for the trip back north.

What about Harriet's father? "Daddy Ben" would be worried sick if he didn't know what happened to his beloved children. Fortunately Daddy Ben, unlike Old Rit, could contain his excitement well enough to not set off the slave masters. She sent a message for him to come to the shed without telling Old Rit. He was there in no time. Harriet and the boys looked at their father. He looked normal except for one thing—his eyes were closed and his head was turned away. Harriet received a very long embrace from her father, as they had not seen each other in quite some time. Still Daddy Ben had not opened his eyes.

The Underground Railroad *(cont.)*

He said a prayer for their safe return voyage north. Still Daddy Ben had not opened his eyes. As he turned to exit the shed, he said, "I must truthfully tell Master that this day, I have not seen you." Harriet, her three brothers, and their families set out for the northerly trek. On this journey, with their father's blessing, they encountered no problems. While back home, Harriet formulated a plan to bring out the two most important slaves of all to her—Daddy Ben and Old Rit. She would have to work to save money for supplies. A key change that had occurred in the United States was going to make her plan a bit more difficult. In 1850, a harsh new fugitive slave law had been passed that permitted any slave who had escaped to a free state to be captured and taken to his or her southern home state, if their old master swore that the slave belonged to them. This only meant that slaves were not safe anywhere in America. Where else could they go? They couldn't afford to take a boat to Europe, and who would want to go that far away from family?

Canada seemed like the best place. They could cross the border without problem. It wasn't much further away from the old Maryland plantation. Canada would have to be the place. Harriet set out for yet another trip down south. When she arrived at the plantation and sent word to her mother and father that it was time to flee to the North, she learned that her father was jailed for allegedly aiding the escape of other slaves. Daddy Ben was in an old wooden "slammer."

38

The Underground Railroad *(cont.)*

Harriet coerced a courageous slave into sawing through that same night. She commanded her parents to leave all but their most precious belongings. They didn't have much anyway. An old friend gave them an old horse with which to pull a buggy. However, they didn't have a buggy or wagon. That night, Harriet gathered old wood from the property and headed for the shed. Luckily, she found some old wagon wheels; she hoped they would last at least until Wilmington, where her parents would catch a Canada-bound train. Harriet would drive alone from Wilmington to the rendezvous spot— Philadelphia. Once together, they would ride the last leg into Canada.

Harriet Tubman would make about twenty more trips that were equally as daring to the South. In all, she led more than 300 slaves to freedom—never losing a single soul, including her own family. During the Civil War, she was a nurse, cook, and spy for the Union army. In 1863, the Emancipation Proclamation was passed, granting freedom to slaves as soon as the Union Army conquered the Southern Confederate states. After the Civil War, Harriet's parents were brought from Canada to live with Harriet in New York. Harriet's ultimate dream—freedom for all slaves—was granted when the Thirteenth Amendment, which absolutely outlawed slavery, was ratified in 1865. Harriet Tubman died in 1913. In her later years, Harriet cared for her parents as well as the elderly and spoke out for women's and black rights.

Questions

1. How did Harriet escape from slavery?
2. How did Harriet fool her former master into not recognizing her?
3. How did Harriet travel from the North to the South and back again?
4. What did Harriet do if a baby cried while they were hiding?
5. Did Harriet's husband wait for her return? What did he do?
6. How do you think Harriet felt when she learned of her husband's marriage?
7. Why did Harriet have to rush to get her brothers?
8. Describe the emotions that Old Rit, Harriet's mother, must have had on Christmas day.
9. How did Harriet get her parents all the way to Canada? Be sure to tell all the modes of transportation used.
10. How would you describe Harriet? List qualities and adjectives.
11. Did Harriet stop helping people after the Civil War? If so, how?
12. List all the ways Harriet helped people.

Acrostic Poem

An acrostic poem is a poem that is based off a word or words. The word(s) is written downward on the page, and words that describe it are attached to the word's letters. For example, if you choose the word *slavery*, you need to think of descriptive words or phrases about slavery.

Example:

Slaves were ⅗ a person

Lots of work to do

A beating was a punishment

Valued by their masters

Everyone ended up free

Directions: Using all of the knowledge you have learned about slavery and some specific people and events in slavery, create an acrostic poem in the space below utilizing one of the following words.

- emancipation
- Dred Scott
- Booker T. Washington

- Harriet Tubman
- Harriet Jacobs
- plantation

- *Amistad*
- Civil War
- Underground Railroad

Slavery from the Beginning

Directions: Read the following excerpt on slavery through the ages and then see what you learned by playing the game on page 42.

Slavery is certainly not a new institution. It can be traced back to the Old Testament of the Bible, 1350 B.C., and ancient Greek and Roman society. Many different nations and peoples have been involved in slavery throughout the ages.

In the ancient history of the Old Testament, slaves were held under the Law of Moses, but all slaves were eventually freed. If a free man was enslaved, the master would be killed. Fathers often sold their daughters. Likewise, debtors and their families were sold into slavery because of their debt. The slaves would be freed after a short time if the master believed their debt was paid off from the work they did. Poor slaves that sold themselves for profit could be bought back by their families or by themselves once they had earned enough money. Slavery in this ancient time was much more forgiving than the systems that were to come.

In Ancient Greece and Rome, prisoners of war were held as slaves for ransom. In Greece, however, once a person was a slave, their children were born slaves. A Greek slave could purchase his freedom with his savings, called a peculium, if his owner agreed. Greek slaves were usually white, like their owners, and therefore, it was difficult to tell the owner apart from the slave.

In Rome, slaves were mainly captured in war. Roman slaves worked alongside their masters under relatively good conditions. They were often treated as tenants on the land of their owners. Roman law did give the master full power over his slaves and even allowed the master to kill his slaves. Slaves were not allowed to own property under this system. Slaves were also not allowed to be married under the law. As Rome developed and became a powerful country, their system of slavery changed.

Under the Roman Empire, there were two types of slaves: house slaves and slaves that worked in the fields (much like American plantation slaves). Soon slave trading became very popular in Italy, and the population of the slaves grew. Eventually, emancipating the slaves became more common and a freed slave would take the name of his master. When Christianity spread to the Empire, it comforted slaves and encouraged better treatment of slaves. Under the Christian Empire, freed slaves were full citizens. It took many years for slavery to end in Rome, but in 377 A.D., the sale of slaves was forbidden.

Although slavery was forbidden in Rome, the system of serfdom originated in Greece and Rome. Serfdom was not slavery but based on classes of people. Certain people had an advantage in society because they had wealth and a lot of land. Serfs did not have any possessions. Serfs were forced to work for the higher class, and they were then allowed to work a small plot of land to grow food to feed themselves and their family. Serfdom soon spread to other parts of Europe, especially Great Britain.

Throughout time there have been slaves in Europe, Asia, Turkey, Morocco, West Africa, Portugal, Spain, Brazil, and the United States to name a few. Slavery is a common theme throughout time. It cannot be easily understood, but it must be so that the same mistakes are not made again. Even today, there are rumors of slavery in parts of Africa and the Middle East. When will we as a human race learn that slavery is no answer?

Origins of Slavery Game

Play of the Game: There are three categories that the student contestants may choose from (as seen below). The students will be divided into two teams. The teacher will act as the game show host and then choose a student from the first team to choose a category. The questions will be ranked in order of points from lowest to highest. The student may choose any category in any amount from 5 to 25 points. Once a category amount is chosen, the teacher will read the answer and the student must respond with a question—much like the game show *Jeopardy*. If the student is unable to cite a question, then the other team is given a chance. Whomever answers with the correct question receives the points valued to that question. The play is continued until all the categories have been answered, and the team with the highest points wins.

*Tip—It may be helpful to place the categories onto an overhead projector or write them on the board so the students can see their choices.

General Slavery	Greek Slavery	Roman Slavery
5	5	5
10	10	10
15	15	15
20	20	20
25	25	25

Questions *(For teacher to see only):*

General Slavery

5—The earliest forms of slavery can be traced back in this book.

10—This nation of people held slaves under the Law of Moses.

15—The person who owned slaves was called this.

20—There are rumors of slavery today in these two places.

25—This was the cause of most slaves and their families being sold into slavery.

Greek Slavery

5—Freedom could be purchased with this in the Greek system.

10—In this country, slaves were mostly white like their owners.

15—Prisoners of war were held as slaves for this.

20—Greece and this country captured slaves as prisoners of war.

25—Greece is located on this continent.

Roman Slavery

5—Masters were allowed to kill their slaves in this country.

10—The spread of this brought better treatment to slaves.

15—In Rome, like the United States, there were these two types of slaves.

20—The sale of slaves was forbidden in Rome in this year.

25—This name was taken on when a slave was freed.

Dred Scott

Dred Scott was born into slavery in the early 1800s. In 1830, Dred and his master, Peter Blow, settled in Missouri. Soon after, Dred was sold to a U.S. army doctor named John Emerson. Scott lived with Dr. Emerson in Missouri until 1834. They then moved to Fort Armstrong in Illinois. Dr. Emerson was not happy there and requested a transfer. The transfer was accepted, and they moved to Fort Snelling in Wisconsin. At the time, Wisconsin was not yet a state and was largely unsettled. After a year in Wisconsin, Emerson complained of poor health and asked to leave. In 1837, Emerson was transferred to a fort in Louisiana. There he met and married Eliza Sanford. Soon after, Dr. Emerson, his wife, and Dred Scott returned to Fort Snelling in Wisconsin. In 1842, Dr. Emerson finally decided to settle in St. Louis, and he died there in 1843. In his will, he left Dred and Dred's wife, Harriet, to his wife, Eliza.

Dred Scott

Almost three years later, in 1846, Dred and Harriet petitioned a Missouri court for their freedom. He claimed that they were being held illegally as slaves because he had lived for two years in Illinois, a free state. He also pointed out that he lived in Wisconsin, which banned slavery in the 1820 Missouri Compromise. Dred's trial began June 30, 1847. In 1850, after more than two years of arguments, the jury awarded them their freedom. Mrs. Emerson appealed the decision, and the case was reheard in 1852. Judge William Scott of the Missouri Supreme Court turned over the lower court's decision and ruled in favor of Eliza Emerson.

Meanwhile, Roswell M. Field, a Vermonter who hoped to use Dred's case to attack the laws of slavery, contacted Dred. Mrs. Emerson, however, no longer owned Dred. He had been given to her brother, John Sanford who lived in New York. Field told Dred to sue Sanford because New York was a free state. Cases between citizens of different states were heard in the U.S. Federal Courts. In 1853, he filed in U.S. Federal Court, and the trial was unsuccessful. They ruled that Dred was still a slave by Missouri law. The last chance was the Supreme Court of the United States. The case began on February 11, 1856. On March 6, 1857, Chief Justice Taney gave his decision that Dred Scott was not free, he was not a citizen, and the Missouri Compromise was unconstitutional. Another justice, Justice Curtis, disagreed, and thought Dred was a citizen and should be free. However, the first judgment had more support. The Southern slave owners were thrilled, but the Northerners were outraged.

In May 1858, Taylor Blow, a descendant of Dred's original owner, Peter Blow, took possession of Scott and his family and set them free. Dred was only able to enjoy his freedom for a short time. He died on September 17, 1858.

Using the blank time line on page 44, fill in the important events of Dred Scott's life.

Dred Scott *(cont.)*

Important Events in Dred Scott's Life and After His Death

1800s— _____

1820 — _____

1834 — _____

1836 — _____

1837 — _____

1843 — _____

1846 — _____

1850 — _____

1852 — _____

1853 — _____

1856 — _____

1857 — _____

1858 — _____

1860 — Abraham Lincoln is elected president.

1861 — Civil War begins.

1862 — Congress bans slavery from territories.

1863 — Emancipation Proclamation frees slaves.

1864 — Taney dies.

1865 — End of the Civil War.

44

Slavery Among the Cherokee Tribe

Directions: Read the following information about slavery in the Cherokee Nation. Using this information, create questions that a classmate will have to answer. These questions should be formatted to have a short response based on the information below. After you have created at least one question for each fact, make a game board. Be sure to have spaces that make you go back or forward a certain number of spaces when you land on them. Decorate the game board and then use your questions, pennies or buttons as markers, and a die to play the game. Whoever gets the question right can move forward the number of spaces that was rolled. Have fun!

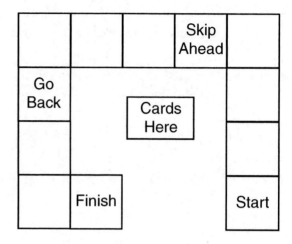

Cherokee Facts

- The Cherokee tribe has been one of the largest and most advanced Indian tribes since the earliest time.

- The Spanish and French used black slaves on the expeditions into Indian country, so Cherokees were introduced to the black man as a servant.

- Some runaway slaves would seek help amongst the Cherokee Nation, but they were treated as intruders and found no aid there.

- Cherokees began possessing black people as slaves for trading purposes.

- The Cherokee Nation had believed in adopting other Indians or white people into their tribe under special circumstances, but they did not believe in adopting a black person.

- The tribe considered African Americans to be an inferior people.

- Southern slave owners were afraid that both African Americans and Indians would join together and revolt against the Southern slave masters, so they deliberately tried to create distrust between the two people.

- There were Cherokee plantation owners who used black slaves, and because of their success, they were role models for other tribal members. The ownership of slaves soon became a mark of status and success in the tribe.

- Cherokees were already slave owners when missionaries first came to their nation. The missionaries accepted slavery and would often borrow or hire the slaves of the Cherokee.

Slavery Among the Cherokee Tribe *(cont.)*

- As the institution of slavery grew, the Cherokee nation developed a slave code to prevent the slaves from running away, rising against their master, and other types of revolt.

- The work of the Cherokee's slaves mostly was in agriculture: they cleared land, built fences, and planted and harvested crops.

- The female slaves were called "mammies" and taught their mistresses how to spin fabrics.

- Most of the slaves lived in windowless log huts with dirt floors and chimneys made of sticks and mud.

- The slaves usually had to carry passes when they were away from home, and they wore clothing similar to the Southern plantation slaves.

- Slave families were often separated by sale. Younger slaves were called "boy" and "girl" while older slaves were called "uncle" and "aunt."

- Cherokees believed slavery to be a divine institution that was a blessing to both slave and master.

- Within the Cherokee Nation, there was never an "underground railroad" operating to free slaves.

- Slaves were used frequently as something to barter and trade with. They were also used as interpreters and business consultants.

- Many Cherokee slaves did not speak English; they spoke Cherokee and their native tongue.

- Cherokees never felt they needed to justify slavery, nor did they feel it was immoral. They believed it was justified because the masters received many benefits from it and that was enough. Unlike the white community, there seems to be little guilt among the Cherokee today.

- Slave stealing was a problem in the nations; other tribes would try to steal the slaves.

- Just before the Civil War, there was an anti-slavery group called the Keetowah Society that rallied against the ownership of slaves and especially the large Cherokee slaveholders.

- It is reported that Cherokee treatment of black slaves was very lenient, and this resulted in discipline problems within the tribe.

The Emancipation Proclamation

Whereas on the 22nd day of September, A.D. 1862, a proclamation was issued by the President of the United States, containing, among other things the following, to wit:

"That on the 1st day of January, A.D. 1863, all persons held as slaves within any State or designated part of a State the people whereof shall then be in rebellion against the United States shall be then, thenceforward, and forever free; and the executive government of the United States, including the military and naval authority thereof, will recognize and maintain the freedom of such persons and will do no act or acts to repress such persons, or any of them, in any efforts they make for their actual freedom.

"That the executive will on the 1st day of January aforesaid, by proclamation, designate the States and parts of States, if any, in which the people thereof, respectively, shall then be in rebellion against the United States; and the fact that any State of the people thereof shall on that day be in good faith represented in the Congress of the United States by members chosen thereto at elections wherein a majority of the qualified voters of such States shall have participated in the absence of strong countervailing testimony, be deemed conclusive evidence that such State and the people thereof are not then in rebellion against the United States."

Now, therefore, I, Abraham Lincoln, President of the United States, by virtue of the power in me vested as Commander-In-Chief of the Army and Navy of the United States, in time of actual armed rebellion against the authority and government of the United States, and as fit and necessary war measure for suppressing said rebellion, do, on this 1st day in January, A.D. 1863, and in accordance with my purpose so to do, publicly proclaimed for the full period of one hundred days from the first day above mentioned, order and designate as the States and parts of States wherein the people thereof, respectively, are this day in rebellion against the United States the following, to wit:

Arkansas, Texas, Louisiana (except the parishes of St. Bernard, Palquemines, Jefferson, St. John, St. Charles, Ascension, Assumption, Terrebone, Lafourche, St. Mary, St. Martin, and Orleans including the city of New Orleans), Mississippi, Alabama, Florida, Georgia, South Carolina, North Carolina, and Virginia (except the forty-eight counties designated as West Virginia, and also the counties of Berkeley, Accomas, Northhampton, Elizabeth City, York, Princess Anne, and Norfolk, including the cities of Norfolk and Portsmouth), and which excepted parts are for the present left as if this proclamation were not issued.

And by virtue of the power and for the purpose aforesaid, I do order and declare that all persons held as slaves within said designated States and parts of States are, and henceforward shall be, free; and that the Executive Government of the United States, including the military and naval authorities thereof, will recognize and maintain the freedom of said persons.

And I hereby enjoin upon the people so declared to be free to abstain from all violence, unless in necessary self-defense; and I recommend to them that, in all cases when allowed, they labor faithfully for reasonable wages.

And I further declare and make known that such persons of suitable condition will be received into the armed service of the United States to garrison forts, positions, stations, and other places, and to man vessels of all sorts in said service.

And upon this act, sincerely believed to be an act of justice, warranted by the Constitution upon military necessity, I invoke the considerate judgment of mankind and the gracious favor of Almighty God.

The Emancipation Proclamation *(cont.)*

Directions

The following Emancipation Proclamation was written to be enforced beginning in 1863. After reading the Emancipation Proclamation, answer the questions that follow.

Questions

1. What did The Emancipation Proclamation do for the situation of the slaves?

   _____

   _____

   _____

   _____

2. Who were the "States, in which the people thereof, . . . shall be in rebellion"?

   _____

   _____

   _____

3. Why was The Emancipation Proclamation a "fit and necessary" war measure?

   _____

   _____

   _____

   _____

4. President Lincoln encourages the freed slaves to abstain from violence. Why do you think he does this, and who would they possibly be violent toward?

   _____

   _____

   _____

   _____

5. Finally, President Lincoln encourages the freed slaves to join the military. Do you think The Emancipation Proclamation was created soley for the freedom of the slaves or also to benefit the Union in fighting the Civil War? Why or why not?

   _____

   _____

   _____

   _____

Frederick Douglass

Frederick Douglass was born in 1818, a slave in Maryland. He escaped from slavery in 1838. He ran first to New York and later moved to Massachusetts. Douglass did not have any formal education. He taught himself how to read and write. He was a powerful speaker, and in 1841, he spoke at a meeting sponsored by the abolitionists. His looks and ability to speak, held his audiences' attention incredibly well. Douglass was soon a famous speaker in the anti-slavery movement. In 1845, he spoke in England to a sympathetic audience in which he enlisted their support for the abolition of slavery in America. Many did not believe that he was a former slave because of his tremendous speaking abilities.

Frederick Douglass

Upon his return from England, he became the leading African-American spokesperson in the anti-slavery movement. He began working for the Underground Railroad, assisting many slaves to escape to the North and then to Canada. In order to have his voice heard by more people, he published the *North Star.* It soon became the most influential paper in the African-American community. Douglass also helped recruit African-American men to fight in the Civil War. He served his country as Secretary of the Santo Domingo Commission, Marshal and Recorder for the Deeds of the District of Columbia, and Minister of the United States of America in Haiti. He also wrote three autobiographies during his life.

Discussion Questions:

- Was Frederick Douglass a typical slave? Did he accomplish what most slaves accomplished in their lifetimes?
- What do you think was his greatest accomplishment? Why?
- If you were a slave during Frederick Douglass's time, would you consider him to be a hero?
- Do you think there were many black heroes with whom the slaves could aspire to be like?
- Why do you think Frederick Douglass recruited African-American men to fight in the Civil War?
- If you were a black man during the Civil War and you were able, would you have fought? Why or why not?
- Name some of the ways in which Frederick Douglass was able to influence others regarding their views of slavery.
- Do you think it was common for an escaped slave to be able to read, write, and be an excellent speaker?

Enrichment: Look up one or all of Frederick Douglass's autobiographies in the library and find out more about his fascinating life.

Narrative of the Life of Frederick Douglass, an American Slave written by himself (Bedford Books, 1993)

My Bondage and My Freedom (Library of America, 1996) Life and Times of Frederick Douglass

Debate

Student Directions:

Prior to and during the Civil War, there were two different viewpoints regarding slavery. First, the abolitionists were strongly against slavery. They wanted the slaves to have the freedoms that they enjoyed and believed all mankind should be free. The Confederates, on the other hand, were pro-slavery. They advocated slavery because many of them believed it was supporting the economics of the South. Some also believed that black people were not true human beings and slavery was their calling in life. Using the books read throughout the unit, *To Be A Slave* and *Letters from a Slave Girl,* and any other resource material on slavery, research the viewpoint that your teacher assigns you. Fill in the chart below to begin your research.

	Abolitionists	Confederates
Who?		
What did they represent?		
Where were they in the U.S.?		
Why did they believe what they did?		

Teacher Directions:

Assign half of the students to be abolitionists and the other half to be Confederates. Have the students research their particular point of view, using the encyclopedia and resources listed in the bibliography. Have them write down quotes from actual slaves or confederates and three to four strong points that they feel represents their group.

Divide the class in half so that the abolitionists are on one side of the class and the confederates are on the other. Face their desks so they are able to look at one another directly. You will stage the debate, giving an introduction to both sides and explaining that you are there to hear the varying viewpoints on the issue of slavery. Start at one end and let a student from the confederate side speak. After that student has spoken, allow a student from the abolitionist side to respond and so forth.

Following the debate, lead a discussion explaining why both groups felt strongly about their viewpoints. Ask the students: Why do you think the confederates/abolitionists were so convinced that their way was the only way? Have the students write a one-paragraph reflection on how they felt during the debate and what they learned from the experience.

Enrichment:

Create a chart from your debate group that depicts the differences between the confederates and abolitionists.

Create a play in which there are both Confederates and abolitionists and act out discussions or disputes they may have.

6666

66666

666666666666666666

Amistad

Social Studies

In 1839, the slave ship *Amistad* set sail from Havana, Cuba. The ship was headed for Puerto Principe. Along the way, however, the captive slaves rebelled against their captors. A man called Senghe Pieh led them. The rebels killed the captain and seized control of the ship. They attempted to sail to Africa but ended up in the United States, instead. Once they arrived there, they were imprisoned and put on trial. As the case unfolded, this "slave rebellion" turned out to be much more complicated. These men had never been slaves—they had been illegally kidnapped from Africa. It took three long years, but eventually, they were able to return home.

© Teacher Created Resources, Inc.　　　51　　　#2613 Thematic Unit—Slavery

Amistad (cont.)

Map of the Voyage of the Amistad

Directions: Using the following information and the map below, label the journey of the Africans. Use three different colored pencils to trace the journeys of the three ships. Be sure to make a key.

The Africans were first kidnapped near Sierra Leone on the west coast of Africa and were taken on the *Tecora* to Cuba. From Cuba, they were put on the *Amistad* and eventually wound up on the east coast of the United States. After three years of trials, they were allowed to return home on the *Gentleman* to Lomboko Harbor near Mendeland.

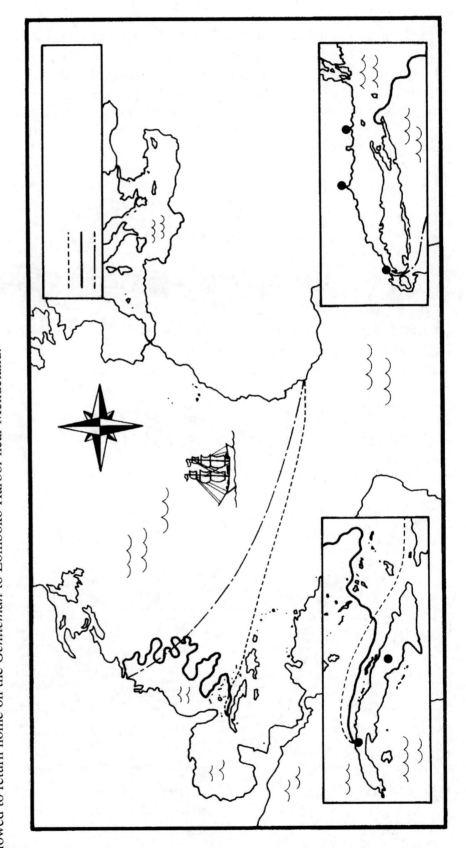

Booker T. Washington

Directions: Use the following Web sites to search the topic "Booker T. Washington." As you find information, take notes about his life and accomplishments. Once you have finished your Internet research, write a one-page biography on Booker T. Washington.

Your biography should include Booker T. Washington's accomplishments, a brief history of his life, and anything you find particularly interesting about him. You may only spend 45–60 minutes on the Web, and you may not go to any other Web site besides those listed below.

(**Note:** all the Web site addresses start with *http://*)

Booker T. Washington

Web sites:

Booker T. Washington
   lcweb2.loc.gov/ammem/aap/bookert.html

History of Booker T. Washington
   www.hal-pc.org/~fdw/btwinf.html

School of Speech
   douglass.speech.nwu.edu/mill_a66.htm

Murray African-American Pamphlets
   ac.acusd.edu/History/WW2Timeline/HOYT/expospeech.html

Creative Quotes from Booker T. Washington
   www.bemorecreative.com/one/40.htm

Booker T. Washington—The Great Accommodator
   people.csnet.net/egy/washington.html

Booker T. Washington—Freedom Through Faith and Labor
   www.capitalresearch.org/crc/pcs/pcs-a996.html

Up from Slavery
   205.230.36/blurbs/Was00100.htm

Virginia—Booker T. Washington National Monument
   outside.starwave.com/npf/VA/2.html

Booker T. Washington—Photo
   www.ferris.edu/htmls/academics/departments/english/jacksonl/boroke.htm

Booker T. Washington—Educator
   www.triadntr.net/~rdavis/bio.htm#booker

Who Was It?

Directions: Match the description on the right with the person or event on the left. There may be more than one description for each event or person.

1. _____ Harriet Tubman

2. _____ Dred Scott

3. _____ *Amistad*

4. _____ Harriet Jacobs

5. _____ Frederick Douglass

6. _____ Booker T. Washington

7. _____ Emancipation Proclamation

8. _____ Underground Railroad

9. _____ Civil War

a. This was a famous slave ship.

b. He made up a last name when he went to school.

c. She rescued her brothers from slavery on Christmas day.

d. He sued his owner for freedom.

e. The slaves rebelled and took over this ship.

f. She hid for years for her freedom.

g. He taught himself to read and write.

h. She was called "Moses."

i. This document was written by Abraham Lincoln.

j. This was a means of escape for slaves.

k. She wrote letters secretly.

l. He gave a speech on the abolition of slavery in England.

m. He was freed from slavery at age nine.

n. This document freed the slaves.

o. This organization had "conductors."

p. It ended slavery in 1865.

q. She eventually rescued her entire family.

r. It involved the Union and the Confederate states.

s. The Africans tried to sail back to Africa but ended up in the United States.

t. The end of this war marked the official end of slavery.

Learning a Lesson

Slaves worked very hard and never reaped the benefits of their labor. They were expected to work very long hours, sometimes from dawn to dusk. Oftentimes, they would work for these long periods of time with very little food and water. After their long day of toil, they would return to their quarters and have to cook dinner and complete the household chores. All this was done without any pay, only a shack in which to live, and scraps to eat.

The concept of such fruitless work is foreign to most children today. Have students complete the activity and the reflection below.

Activity: For one week, inform your students that they will be picking up litter around the school for five minutes every day. Tell them that they will be paid in fake money for their work and on Friday there will be a store in which they can buy treats with their earnings. Complete the activity as planned, and give the students their fake salary at the end of each day. On Friday, however, call the students up one at a time and ask the total amount they earned and then take the money from them. After each student has had their salary taken back, tell them there will be no treats. The students will obviously be upset and then you can explain that this is how slaves must have felt in their lives. The students worked hard like slaves, and in the end they received nothing for their labor. Ask the students how they felt when they realized they weren't getting anything in exchange for their work. Ask them to reflect on how slaves must have felt reaping nothing from their labor for a lifetime.

Reflection: Draw a symbol or picture that you believe represents slavery. Around the picture write six to eight adjectives describing how slaves must have felt and how you felt when you realized that you weren't going to receive a reward for your work.

Build a Machine

Slave masters had high expectations for their slaves in all areas. They were expected to work extremely hard. This was especially true for the field slaves who picked cotton. These slaves were expected to pick at least 250 pounds (115 kg) of cotton a day. If this quota was not met, they were severely beaten. If the slaves had some sort of invention, they would have had a much easier time meeting their quotas.

Creating a Machine

1. Divide the class into groups of four or five students.

2. Instruct the students that they will be making a machine using all of their bodies working together. The machine will reduce the time of picking cotton and make the task easier on the slaves. Each person in the group will be in charge of a different part or action of the machine.

3. Instruct the students that in order to make the entire machine work, they must work together and be in the appropriate order.

4. The students should be given time to create and perfect their machine. Once they are finished, each group will demonstrate their machine to the class. Each group must be able to explain their machine and the specific functions it performs.

5. Ask questions like: What is each action for? Why did you use that action? How would this machine make picking cotton easier? Why do you think the slaves didn't make a machine? If they did, do you think their master would have used it? Why or why not? Was it difficult to work together and create one machine? Were there many different ideas on how to start and what to make? How did you decide which one to use? Were you pleased with the way your machine turned out? Why or why not?

Variation

1. Divide the class in half, and have half the students create the machines away from the others.

2. Have the other half of the class write down ideas and discuss what would be important.

3. Once the time limit is up for creating the machines, compare the ideas of the two groups.

4. Ask the machine group to demonstrate their machines and the discussion groups to present what they talked about.

5. Discuss with the students which was more effective in creating a machine. Why is it important to experiment with new inventions and try things out?

Enrichment: Research Eli Whitney and the cotton gin and compare your machine to his. Draw a diagram of a real machine that would pick cotton.

Grow Your Own Cotton

Cotton was and still is a very popular crop grown in the South. The slaves had to be very familiar with the growth of the cotton plant in order to be successful at harvesting the cotton. You will be able to experience a small part of the agricultural work of the slaves by growing your own cotton plant.

Directions for Growing Cotton

1. Obtain seeds for cotton plants from a local nursery or agricultural center.

2. Each student will need a cup, one or two cottonseeds, half a cup of fertilized soil, and a craft stick.

3. The students will plant the cotton by placing a fourth of a cup of the soil into the cup and then placing the seeds on top of the soil. The seeds should be covered with the remaining soil and then watered a small amount (approximately one tablespoon) every three days. Then have the students write their name on their craft stick and put it in the cup. The plants will take approximately four to six weeks to sprout, so it is recommended that this activity be done at the beginning or before the unit begins.

4. Throughout the unit, the students should be required to keep a journal on the growth of their plant. They should record the growth of the plant once it sprouts by measuring it daily. In addition, they should record any changes in the plant and any other observations they make.

5. Once a green bowl has appeared, the student may stop measuring but should continue watering until the white cotton puff appears. The student may pick the cotton and take the plant home.

Enrichment: The students may complete a line graph demonstrating the growth of the cotton throughout the unit.

Slave Quarters

Typical field slaves lived in the slave quarters on the plantation. The conditions of these quarters varied but they were often quite undesirable. Read the excerpt below taken from *African Americans Voices of Triumph; Perseverance* (published by Time-Life Books, Alexandria, Virginia, 1993.)

At night, field-slave families crowded into small one- or two-room cabins. Each of which were able to hold twelve people. The cabins were sweltering hot in summer; in winter, when the cold wind whistled through the walls, slaves huddled together for warmth. (The one-room cabin could have had dimensions of 10½ feet by 10½ feet (3.2m x 3.2m). The distance from the floor to the ceiling may have been up to 8 feet (2.9m). If there was furniture, it consisted mainly of wooden benches and chairs. Slaves made mattresses of straw or moss, and every third year or so they would receive a new cotton blanket from their masters.

Directions:

Using the pieces of the model cabin on pages 59 and 60, create your own model of the slave quarters. Be sure to make two sides and two ends. Glue the sides and ends together. Then cut out a door and windows as you wish. Cut the roof out of construction paper to fit and decorate the cabin as you like. After you have constructed the cabin, answer the questions on page 61.

Slave Quarters *(cont.)*

Model of side of cabin

Teacher Directions: Make two copies of this page for each student.

Scale: 1 inch = 1½ feet

Slave Quarters *(cont.)*

Model of front and back of cabin

Teacher Directions: Make two copies for each student.

Scale: 1 inch = 1½ feet

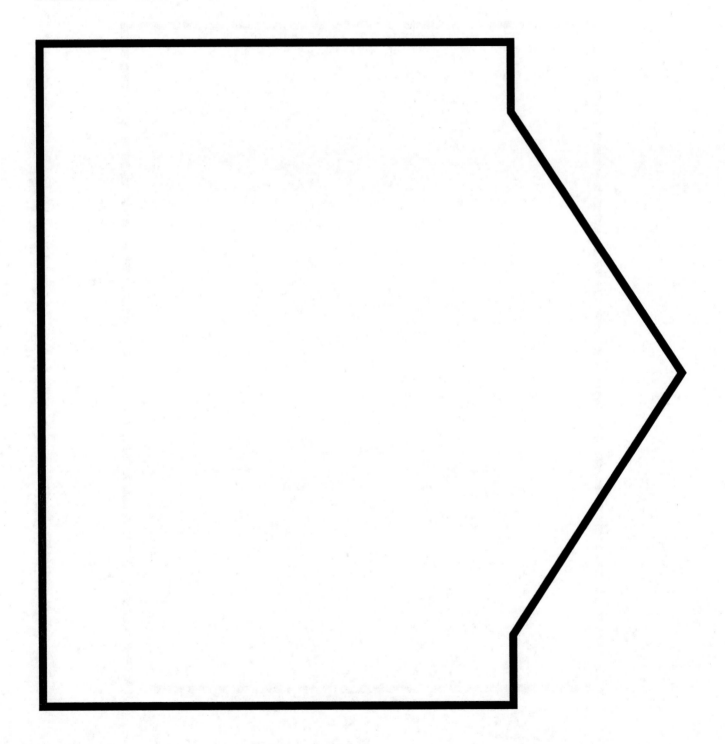

60

Slave Quarters and Dimensions

Answer the following questions and be sure to show your work in the space below each question.

1. The cabin you have created has one room with the dimensions of 10½ feet x 10½ feet (3.2 m x 3.2 m). Draw a model including the dimensions of that room. What is the perimeter of the one room cabin? (Remember, the perimeter is the total distance around the outside.)

2. If the cabin has dimensions of 10 feet x 12 feet (3 m x 3.7 m), find the area of the one room cabin.

3. What would the perimeter of the cabin be if the room was 35 feet x 8 feet (10.7 m x 2.5 m)?

4. What would the area be if the dimensions were 6 feet x 23 feet (1.8 m x 7 m)? Is that a large cabin compared to the other two?

5. If a slave family had a two-room cabin and the first room is 45 feet x 3 feet (13.8 m x 9 m) and the second room is 5 feet x 4 feet (1.5 m x 1.2 m), what is the total area of that cabin? What is the perimeter of each room added together?

6. Would you rather live in a cabin that was 10 feet x 13 feet (3 m x 4 m) or 35 feet x 6 feet (10.8 m x 1.8 m)? Why? Please show your calculations of the areas.

7. Would you rather live in a cabin that had a larger perimeter or larger area? Why?

Underground Railroad

Map of the Underground Railroad

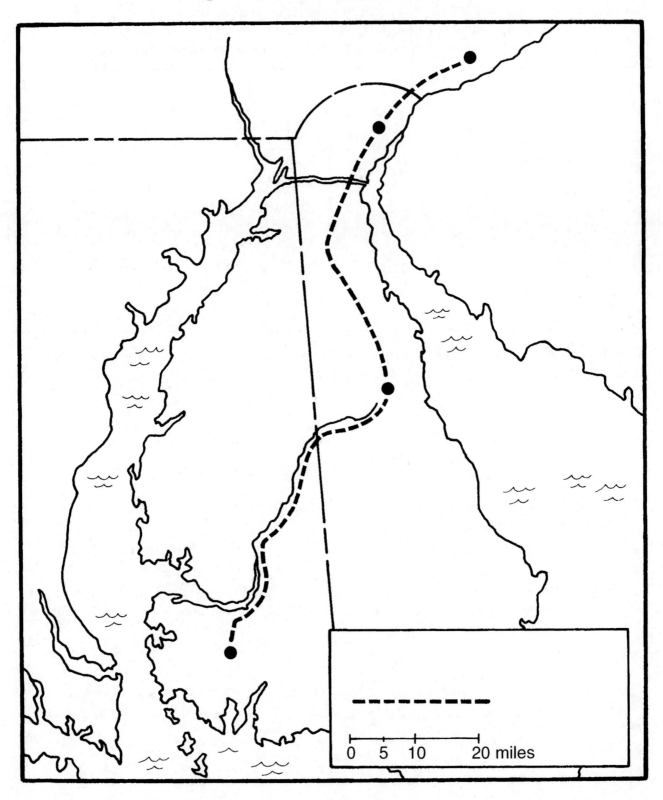

0   5   10   20 miles

Underground Railroad *(cont.)*

Directions: Using a green, blue, and red colored pencil and the map on page 62, complete the following tasks.

Section 1:

1. Using your red colored pencil, trace Harriet's journey on the Underground Railroad.

2. Using your green colored pencil, circle Harriet's starting point and final destination.

3. Using your blue colored pencil, outline the river that borders on Harriet's journey.

Section 2:

Using the map and the scale, solve the following problems. Please show your work.

1. Calculate the distance from Bucktown to Camden.

2. Calculate the number of miles from Camden to Wilmington.

3. Calculate the distance from Wilmington to Philadelphia.

4. Calculate the total distance Harriet traveled. (Remember, you can use your answers from numbers 1–3.)

5. If Harriet were to travel for two hours at a time, at a rate of 1 mile per hour, how far would she travel every two hours?

6. If Harriet were to travel a total of 200 miles and she traveled 3 miles a day, how many days would the trip take her?

7. Harriet traveled 6 miles on day one, 3 miles on day two, 4 miles on day three, and 7 miles on day four. What is the average number of miles traveled in a day?

8. If 300 people escape by the Underground Railroad and they each traveled 150 miles, how many miles were traveled altogether?

9. If Harriet were traveling north from Camden, how many miles away is the next town? What is it?

10. If Harriet is in Philadelphia and she travels to the southernmost town, what town is it? How many miles away is it?

Slavery Information

There are many different ways to portray information. When numbers are being compared, the use of a graph is most efficient. There are three popular graphs: circle graph (pie chart), bar graph, and line graph.

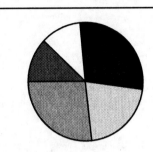

A **circle graph** is best used to compare five to six items in relation to themselves based on the sizes of the slices of the circle or pie.

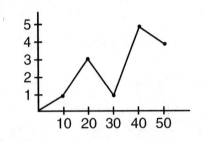

A **line graph** shows trends over time.

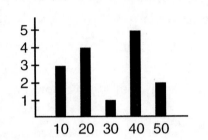

A **bar graph** shows comparison in a concrete fashion.

Directions: Using graph paper, the above information on graphs, and the following facts, create the graphs below.

The slave population grew in the South from less than 700,000 in 1790 to more than two million by 1830. By 1860, the number of slaves had doubled to four million.

1. Create a bar graph using the population and dates.

2. Create a line graph that shows the difference over time in the population by dates.

On many cotton plantations, slaves were whipped for not picking their share of the crop, usually 1,500 pounds a week.

3. Create a circle graph (pie chart) in the space below that shows how much Joe picked for the week by daily amounts.

   Joe picked:

   Day 1—260 lbs.

   Day 2—190 lbs.

   Day 3—245 lbs.

   Day 4—200 lbs.

   Day 5—350 lbs.

   Day 6—125 lbs.

A Riddle for Freedom

Introduction: Slaves often created riddles, songs, and puzzles as part of their oral tradition. The following scene is a dramatic reenactment of one which occurred on few plantations. Keep in mind that this plantation has a fair master that keeps his word to the slave, and this is not necessarily an accurate portrayal of history. This activity allows students to participate in a dramatic depiction of an oral history.

Directions: Read the script aloud with each student taking turns reading a part. Once the story has been read once or twice, select students to act out the parts of Sam, Master Brian, and the narrator.

A Riddle for Freedom

Narrator: Now there was a man called Sam who was a slave in Georgia that I met when I was working as a field slave in the cotton fields. One Christmas morning, Sam knocked on the Big House, and Master Brian Benjamin came out on the porch.

Sam: Good morning, Master.

Master Brian: Good morning, Sam.

Narrator: Now on this particular plantation there was a Christmas tradition that the slaves would approach the master and say . . .

Sam: Christmas gift, Master?

Master Brian: You got me, Sam! You said Christmas gift first, so what would you like to have?

Sam: My freedom, Master. If I can tell you a riddle that you can't solve, will you give me my freedom?

Narrator: Master Brian thought about this for a few minutes and thought there was no way his slave could be smarter than he and said . . .

Master Brian: Sure, Sam, tell me a riddle.

Narrator: Now Sam didn't tell Master Brian the riddle right away. A whole year passed and it was Christmas day again. Sam rode up to big house on a young colt and knocked on the door. When Master Brian came out, they bade each other good morning just like the year before.

Sam: Master, would you please ask your family and house servants to join us on the porch and all the field hands. I want them all to hear the riddle I promised you at Christmas this time last year.

Narrator: Master Brian did as Sam asked and soon all were on the porch awaiting Sam's riddle. Sam got back on his horse and began his riddle.

Sam: Bingo, lingo, lang, tang
Chicken he flutters the do lang tang.
Old eighteen hundred and fifty one
To my home in and out
The dead I seen but didn't shout.
Under the gravel I do travel
My feet I say are iron clad,
I ride the one who was never born
And her mama is still her scorn.
Water it soaks up in the man
Not a pollywog to be seen,
Four there were but three there be
As I am a martyr, set me free!

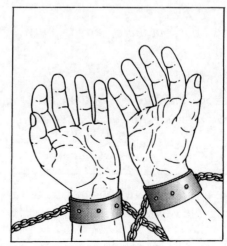

A Riddle for Freedom *(cont.)*

Narrator: Master Brian's face became flustered. He paced the porch. Sam was his best field slave, and he didn't want to lose him. Master stomped his foot on the old wooden boards of the porch, but he just couldn't answer the riddle.

Sam: I'll tell you once more, Master, and if you still can't answer it, then I know you'll give me my freedom because your word is as good as your bond.

Narrator: So Sam told him the riddle one more time. But Master just couldn't figure it out.

Master Brian: Alright Sam, I can't get it. You can have your freedom and that colt, too, as a gift.

Narrator: So after telling the answer, Sam rode off across the field with his freedom papers. And from that day on, he was never a slave anymore.

The Answer:

Bingo, lingo, lang, tang

Chicken he flutters the do lang tang

(That was the introduction)

Old eighteen hundred and fifty-one

(The year it happened)

To my home in and out

The dead I seen but didn't shout

(As Sam went in and out of his quarters, he had seen the skeleton of a horse and he was sure not to scream because that would attract the attention of the overseer)

Under the gravel I do travel

(Sam had dirt on top of his hat, and of course Master Brian couldn't see it)

My feet I say are iron clad

(Sam's feet were in the stirrup irons)

I ride the one who was never born

And her mama is still her scorn

(Jim was riding a colt who was never born because its mother died in labor. Sam had made a whip out of the mother after she died. Of course Master Brian didn't know anything about it)

Water it soaks up in the man

Not a pollywog to be seen

(Sam had water in his boots but there were no pollywogs that the Master could see)

Four there were but three there be

As I am a martyr, set me free!

(Sam's table in his cabin had four legs but one broke leaving three. Sam was a martyr because he suffered in silence and now he wanted to be set free.)

Activity: Write a riddle about yourself and tell it to someone. See if he or she can figure out why you have the clues you do.

Quilts

Slaves often made quilts from scraps of fabric that the master or slaves from the Big House gave to them. The quilts were made for several reasons: to keep the slaves warm, to brighten and decorate their quarters, and sometimes to use as secret maps. The secret maps were used for the Underground Railroad. The fabric would be shaped as landmarks and secret symbols to show the slaves where to go and meet when it was their time to escape.

This activity can be used with the book, *Sweet Clara and the Freedom Quilt* by Deborah Hopkinson (see Bibliography, page 78). The students can use the above information and/or the book to create a quilt.

Materials:

- colored construction paper
- a variety of fabrics and scraps
- glue
- yarn or string

Instructions:

Think about your neighborhood and the landmarks that can be found there. In the area below, lightly draw your map. Show where houses, buildings, streets, trees, and other landmarks are located in your neighborhood. Cut out shapes for houses and buildings using paper or fabric. Dab some glue on the marks you made on the paper and place your cutout shapes there. Remember to add detail so the map will be easy to follow. Try to find materials that will make the map realistic. Once you get home, test your map and have someone in your neighborhood try to find an item on your map.

Enrichment: If you really enjoyed this, create a class quilt. Collect scraps of material and cut a large sheet into squares. Students can sew their own squares with any designs or landmarks they wish. Then ask a parent volunteer to sew the quilt squares together and display the completed quilt on your classroom wall.

Calabash

The calabash is originally associated with Nigeria. A calabash was a decorative item, yet it was also used to store water if an opening was left at the top. A real calabash grows on a vine like a pumpkin or a watermelon, and craftsmen would scoop out the soft inside, then harden the remaining half shells, often by leaving them out in the hot sun or sometimes by baking them. Since they don't grow in North America, the slaves had to find something else to store their water in. The slaves used gourds, which are similar to squash in shape. The same process was used to dry the gourds, and they were then decorated and used for storage. Follow the instructions below to make your own calabash.

Materials:

- newspaper
- balloons
- glue
- water
- sand paper
- pins
- different colored paints
- shellac (optional)

Directions

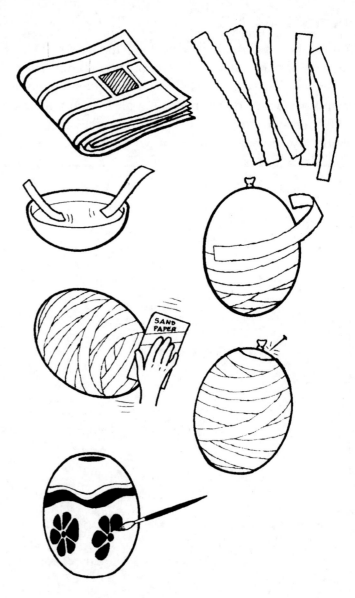

1. Tear newspapers into thin strips.

2. Blow up a few balloons. (The size depends on how big or small you want your calabash to be.)

3. Dip the strips of paper into a bowl of mixed glue and water and shake off excess liquid. Then cover each balloon with several layers of sticky paper. Remember to leave a space at the top for an opening to pour water out of.

4. Let dry for a few hours. If there are rough edges, you can sand them down. Do some extra sanding to form a flat base at the bottom. You can use a sheet of sandpaper. Carefully, using a pin, pop each balloon.

5. You can apply shellac, or for a different look, paint the outside in different colors.

6. Try a different design for each gourd made.

7. Display your gourds around the room.

Reprinted with permission of Simon & Schuster from *JUBA THIS AND JUBA THAT: 100 African-American Games for Children* by Dr. Darlene Powell Hopson and Dr. Derek Hopson, with Thomas Clavin. Copyright © 1996 by Darlene Powell Hopson, Derek S. Hopson, and Thomas Clavin.

Who Owns . . . ?

Slaves were the property of their masters. The idea of one human being owning another is a very controversial idea. Is it right for one person to be free but another to be owned? Many have compared this to owning things of nature. Is it possible or right to own the sun or the wind? If this is impossible or wrong, should human beings be owned?

Discuss as a class what should be owned and what should not. Write the opinions of the students on the board in two categories. Use this for reference once they begin the project.

Student Instructions: Write a rough draft on what you believe shouldn't be owned. The writing will answer the question "Who owns the . . . ?" Explain who or what you believe does own your object and why others or human beings cannot. Your final draft will be written on plain white paper in crayon. You will then paint over the crayon with watercolor. Paint a depiction of what you believe cannot be owned according to what you wrote.

Example:

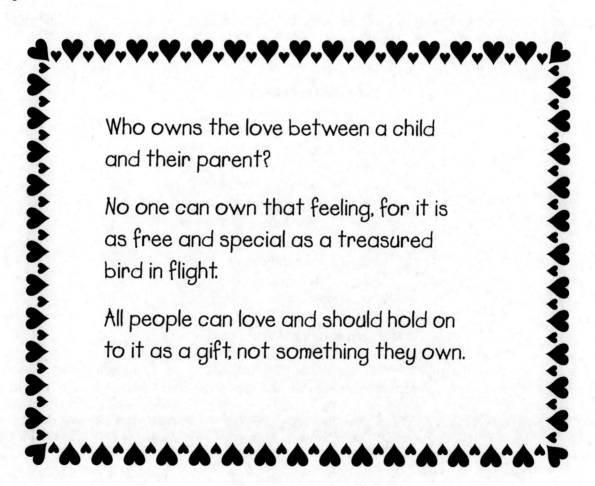

Who owns the love between a child and their parent?

No one can own that feeling, for it is as free and special as a treasured bird in flight.

All people can love and should hold on to it as a gift, not something they own.

Juba This and Juba That

For the most part, African Americans developed this rhyming game in the nineteenth century. Slave or free, many families had to eat whatever was available—leftovers, hand-picked vegetables, ends of meat and bread, "a little of this and a little of that"—and a way to make the meal tasty was to cook or mix all the different ingredients together to produce something new. *Juba* may have been a variation of the word *giblets*, and for a while in New Orleans, in the early 1800s, there was a dance performed by African Americans called the Juba that used a variety of spontaneous movements. This version is reminiscent of that dance, with words added in the following decades.

A student is chosen to be the caller for the song. The caller must make up movements that go along with the words he calls.

At the end of the first line of the song, the players clap once.

At the end of the second line of the song, the players clap twice. The pattern is established: clap once, then twice, then once again, then twice again.

The song can continue indefinitely, as long as the caller can keep inventing rhymes. If he gets stuck, he is replaced by another student. The following traditional chant will help get the class started, but feel free to allow the student to make up their own, if they feel comfortable.

> *Juba this and Juba that.*
> *And Juba kills a yellow cat.*
> *You sift a meal, you give the husk,*
> *You cook the bread, you give me the crust.*
> *You fry the meat, you give me the skin,*
> *And that's where my momma's troubles begin.*
> *Then you Juba*
> *You just Juba.*
> *Juba up, Juba down.*
> *Juba all around the town.*
> *Juba for Ma, Juba for Pa.*
> *Juba for your brother-in-law.*
> *Juba that and Juba this,*
> *I'll keep rhyming, I won't miss.*

Enrichment: Research the kinds of foods the slaves were able to eat. Write a journal entry discussing how you think the slaves felt not getting enough to eat and eating the table scraps from the Big House.

Chinene Nye?

The song game Chinene Nye? or What is big? was played by the people of the Ovimubundu Tribe from the country now called Zimbabwe. Many slaves continued to sing this and other traditional songs to remind them of home. The song uses call and response throughout the game. When call and response is used, a leader calls out a question or phrase and a chorus responds with an answer. There is no set melody or pronunciation; the call and response is called out in a sing-song voice in English or an attempted pronunciation by the class.

Playing the song game:

1. Choose one student to be the song leader. The other students are the chorus. The song begins once the leader calls.

    Leader: Chinene nye? (What is big?)

    Chorus: Chinene on jamba. (Elephant is big.)

    Leader: Chinene nye? (What is big?)

    Chorus: Chinene on jamba. (Elephant is big.)

    Both: Kinyama viosi. (Among all the animals of the world.)
               Ka ku li ukuavo. (There is none larger.)

2. After the chorus and leader repeat the last two lines of the song, the leader chooses another animal, and then another, offering animals that are generally considered big. Here are some examples:

    malanga—cheetah

    ngeve—hippopotamus

    hosi—lion

    ngue—leopard

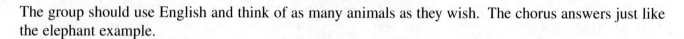

The group should use English and think of as many animals as they wish. The chorus answers just like the elephant example.

3. Now the song leader can be more creative. He can choose to call out the name of an animal that is not considered big, such as shrimp or rat. These should be mixed up with other large animals.

4. Chorus members who respond incorrectly—for example, saying "Mouse is big"—are out, so chorus members must pay attention.

5. The last chorus member remaining calls, "O wi" (song ends) and becomes the new song leader.

Enrichment: Find call and response music from different time periods or cultures and have the class listen to them. Write lyrics for a call and response song that the slaves may have sung with one another during their long days at work.

Reprinted with permission of Simon & Schuster from *JUBA THIS AND JUBA THAT: 100 African-American Games for Children* by Dr. Darlene Powell Hopson and Dr. Derek Hopson, with Thomas Clavin. Copyright © 1996 by Darlene Powell Hopson, Derek S. Hopson, and Thomas Clavin.

The Cat and the Rat

The Cat and the Rat or Kameshi Ne Mpuku is a traditional African game that comes from the Luba tribe in the Congo. Many tribes played various forms of this game, and it was brought to America and played by the slave children. Although there was little time for socializing, the children managed to find time to play even if it was during their chores.

Start of the Game:

The players need to stand in four equal rows so there are three aisles among them. The players in each row hold hands. One player is chosen to be the caller. Two more players are chosen to be the cat and the rat. At a signal by the caller, the rat runs up and down the aisles with the cat in pursuit.

Play of the Game:

As the rat and cat run up and down the aisles, the caller shouts "Mpuki ekale" which means "Let the rat stop." At this call, the players in the rows drop their hands and join hands with the row across. This changes the direction of the aisles, and the rat must adapt to the change or be trapped. At regular intervals, the caller shouts and the aisles change directions. When the rat is caught, two new players are chosen. A time limit can be set. For example, if five minutes pass and the rat has not been captured, he or she wins and can choose the next two players.

Enrichment: After playing the game, the teacher can lead a class discussion on how African slave children must have felt when they came to America and had to work and could no longer be free to play.

Bivoe Ebuma

This game was typically played in the village streets of Angola. Slave children were allowed to play when or where they wanted. This game was played by their ancestors and most likely adapted for slave children to play on plantations.

Start of the Game:

Draw a line in the dirt or with chalk on the pavement that is long enough so the number of students playing can stand on either side in equal rows facing each other. Each row should be about six feet (180 cm) away from the line.

Play of the Game:

A player is selected and begins by making the first toss (with a small ball or piece of fruit). The ball can be thrown to any player on the other side of the line. The ball is kept in play by tossing it from one row to the other. Each time the ball is caught, the other players clap and stamp their feet once. Any player in the row can catch the ball, but no one may step over the line. If a student steps over the line, then he or she must sit out until a new game begins. If the ball is dropped, the one who tossed it throws it again. The game is most exciting if the players try to decrease the time between tosses and the rhythm of clapping and stomping becomes fast.

Reprinted with permission of Simon & Schuster from *JUBA THIS AND JUBA THAT: 100 African-American Games for Children* by Dr. Darlene Powell Hopson and Dr. Derek Hopson, with Thomas Clavin. Copyright © 1996 by Darlene Powell Hopson, Derek S. Hopson, and Thomas Clavin.

My Little Bird

This game is originally from Tanganyika. There is a version that is known in the United States as "Birds Fly." This version is thought to have originated from slaves who played My Little Bird.

Play of the Game:

The players stand together in a group, with the exception of one student who stands apart. The student who was chosen to stand apart from the group calls out, "My little bird is lively," and flaps his arms. Then he quickly calls out the name of another bird or animal, such as "Blue Bird. . . flies!" or "Elephant. . . flies!" and he flaps his arms again. If what the student calls really can fly, the group imitates his flapping arms. If it cannot fly, the players stand still.

Any player who flaps his/her arms in response to the naming of a non-flying animal is out. When all players are out, the game begins again with a new caller.

If only one player is left with the caller, a limit can be set in how many times the caller can try to trick her. For example, if after three tries the remaining player isn't out, she is the winner and takes over as the caller.

Reprinted with permission of Simon & Schuster from *JUBA THIS AND JUBA THAT: 100 African-American Games for Children* by Dr. Darlene Powell Hopson and Dr. Derek Hopson, with Thomas Clavin. Copyright © 1996 by Darlene Powell Hopson, Derek S. Hopson, and Thomas Clavin.

Concluding the Unit on Slavery

Do any of the following activities as a culmination to this fascinating unit on slavery.

1. Ask the students to reflect on what they have learned about slavery in the United States since they first started the unit. Ask them to think of things they still don't know or would like to know more about. On a sheet of paper have them create a KWL chart. Divide the paper into three sections. The first section is labeled "Know," the second is "Want to Know," and the third is "Learned." Have them complete the three sections. Once they are finished, ask them if anyone was surprised by all that they have learned or surprised by how interested they have become in slavery.

2. Give students an opportunity to share items that they have completed during the unit. They may want to share their journals, artwork, or writing assignments. You may invite parents or another class to your sharing time.

Know	Want to Know	Learned

3. Write to the Juneteenth organizations (see Bibliography on page 78) and ask for more information about the origins and celebratory traditions of the holiday. Have your own Juneteenth celebration (page 77).

4. Rent the movie *Uncle Tom's Cabin*. This film is not rated, therefore you will need permission from administration and parents. After the film, ask the students if it was difficult for them to watch slavery when it is associated with real people. Ask them if it was like they imagined. Find out if there was anything they thought wasn't factual.

5. Assist the students in completing "Ruby Bridges" (page 75) and/or Slavery Simulation (page 76).

6. Invite the students to write a paragraph entitled "How Slavery Changed Me." This paragraph should be about the impact that slavery has had on them or their families either through direct experience or learning about it in class. Once they have written their paragraphs, have the students fold the paper in half and create a cover on the outside. Encourage them to draw a picture of an aspect of slavery that really touched them or one they found interesting. They may draw a specific slave or just a general scene.

Ruby Bridges

The Story of Ruby Bridges by Robert Coles discusses the changes that have been made since slavery and in particular, the integration of black students into white schools.

Tell the students that you will be reading a book that discusses some changes since slavery. Ask them to think of some changes in race relations that they know have occurred since slavery and write a list on the board under the title, "Changes Since Slavery."

Then read the book. Refer back to the list that was made before the book was read. Ask the students if the book helped them remember any other changes that have occurred since slavery. Perhaps give some suggestions if they are short on ideas, then . . . .

Make another column on your list and title it "Future Changes." Now ask the students what changes they believe still need to occur between races in today's society. Ask them why they feel these changes are necessary and why they will be helpful. Ask them to make a "How?" column to explain how they are going to contribute to the changes they suggest.

Changes Since Slavery	Future Changes	How?

There are other books that also discuss this period in history. Make them available to the class to share and to stimulate discussion.

Haskins, James. *Separate but not Equal: the Dream and the Struggle.* Scholastic, 1997.

King, Jr., Martin Luther. *I Have A Dream.* Scholastic, 1997.

Myers, Walter Dean. *Young Martin's Promise.* Raintree Steck-Vaughn, 1993.

Patterson, Charles. *The Civil Rights Movement.* Facts on File, 1995.

Rediger, Pat. *Great African-Americans in Civil Rights.* Crabtree Publishing, Co., 1996.

Reef, Catherine. *Ralph David Abernathy.* Dillon Press, 1995.

Slavery Simulation

Directions: As closure to the unit, create a simulation of slavery that allows the student to experience how it felt to be either a slave or a master. As the students enter the room, instruct them to stand in front of the classroom. Once all the students are there, instruct all the students with a particular feature (that the children have no control over, such as eye color) to sit in one section of the room. Once the majority of the students (approximately ¾) are seated, allow the rest of the students to sit in the other section of the room segregated from the first group. Tell the larger group of students that they are slaves who are only considered to be 3/5ths of a person and property of their master. They have no say in the classroom and must listen to the teacher and the smaller group of students all day. They are not allowed to talk back and if they disagree, they will be punished. Inform the smaller group of students that they are plantation owners and they have a voice in the classroom all day. They are allowed to tell the slaves what to do. However, they must remember that slaves do work for them, so they should be nice and polite. (*Note:* It is extremely important that you, as the teacher, are serious throughout the activity and convey this attitude to the class.)

Throughout the day, give preference to the "plantation owners" and treat the "slaves" not as well. For example, allow the "plantation owners" to go to lunch and be dismissed first. For a more dramatic effect, seat the "slaves" in the back of the room. Be sure that the students are playing their roles appropriately and that you make clear what behaviors are not acceptable (i.e., name-calling). Be sure to remind the students that they are playing the role of someone who lived before them and experienced this time period.

Closure:

Lead a discussion with the class that focuses on their feelings about the simulation. Ask the following questions:

- How did the simulation make you feel?

- How did you feel as a "slave" and how were you treated?

- How did it feel to be a "plantation owner" and how did you feel treating the "slaves" the way you did?

- Why do you think the plantation owners of the South treated the slaves with prejudice and believed they weren't humans?

- What do you think the slaves thought about being treated like animals and worked to death?

- Did this activity give you a better understanding of slavery?

- What do you understand more clearly as a result of this activity?

- Do you think this simulation was true to how slavery was or do you think slavery was worse or better? Why?

Juneteenth

Juneteenth, otherwise known as Freedom Day or Emancipation Day, is a very important holiday for African-Americans. Juneteenth originated in Texas. The slaves in Texas had not yet heard the news of the Emancipation Proclamation and their freedom. On June 19, 1865, the news of the Emancipation Proclamation reached Texas two years, six months, and eighteen days late. Some slaves didn't learn about their freedom until even later because their masters didn't tell them. They were hoping to get another crop from the slaves before they spread the news. Once the news of the slaves' freedom was heard, there were celebrations of dancing, singing, and shouting everywhere. That is how the holiday of Juneteenth began. It soon spread to other southwestern states and to the east.

Juneteenth is still celebrated in most states today. The celebration always includes the reading of the Emancipation Proclamation and Proclamation #3 (an abbreviated version of the Emancipation Proclamation). There are parades, picnics, softball games, horseshoes, sack racing, foot racing, tug-o-war, and a cakewalk. Juneteenth is a time to remember how freedom came for slaves in Texas and more importantly, to celebrate that freedom came to all slaves.

Activities:

❑ Create your own Juneteenth celebration to conclude the unit. The date certainly does not have to be June 19. The celebration can be symbolic of the freedom that the slaves were given at the end of a very long trial. Invite the students to bring in foods for the picnic.

  • Before the celebration begins, read the Emancipation Proclamation aloud and ask the students to pretend they are slaves being set free. Ask them how they feel and what they would do at the moment freedom came.

  • Play games like the ones listed above or some of your students' favorite games. This day should be a time of celebration and remembrance.

  • Invite parents to join in on your Juneteenth celebration.

❑ Have the children create a poster board explaining how Juneteenth came to be a holiday and the traditional activities that are part of the celebration.

❑ Parade around the school holding a poster illustrating Juneteenth. Invite other classes to watch your parade. Have the students dress up like former slaves. Create an atmosphere of celebration by playing freedom songs or upbeat African-American music.

Happy Juneteenth

Bibliography

Books:

African American Voices of Triumph: Perserverance. Time-Life Books, 1993.

Amper, Thomas. Booker T. Washington. Carolrhoda Books, Inc., 1998.

Bell, Janet Cheatham. Famous Black Quotations. Warner Books, 1995.

Blockson, Charles L. The Underground Railroad. Prentice Hall Press, 1987.

Branch, Muriel Miller. Juneteenth—Freedom Day. Cobblehill, 1998.

Coles, Robert. The Story of Ruby Bridges. Scholastic, Inc., 1995.

Douglass, Frederick. Escape from Slavery: The Boyhood of Frederick Douglass in His Own Words. Alfred A. Knopf, 1994.

Ferris, Jeri. Go Free or Die: A Story About Harriet Tubman. Carolrhoda Books, Inc., 1988.

Goss, Linda and Clay. Jump Up and Say! A Collection of Black Storytelling. Simon and Schuster, 1995.

Hamilton, Virginia. Many Thousand Gone: African-Americans from Slavery to Freedom. Alfred A. Knopf, 1993.

Hansen, Joyce. Between 2 Fires: Black Soldiers in the Civil War. The African-American Experience. Franklin Watts, 1965.

Hopkinson, Deborah. Sweet Clara and the Freedom Quilt. Alfred A. Knopf, 1993.

Hopson, Dr. Darlene Powell, Dr. Derek S. Hopson, and Thomas Clavin. Juba This and Juba That. Fireside Books, 1996.

January, Brendan. The Dred Scott Decision. Children's Press, 1998.

Katz, William Loren. Breaking the Chains: African-American Slave Resistance. Maxwel MacMillan International Publishing Group, 1990.

Lester, Julius. To Be A Slave. Dial Books for Young Readers, 1968.

Lyons, Mary E. Letters from a Slave Girl: The Story of Harriet Jacobs. Charles Scribner's Sons, 1992.

Mabee, Carleton. Sojourner Truth: Slave, Prophet, Legend. University Press, 1993.

McKissak, Patricia and Frederick. The Story of Booker T. Washington. Children's Press, Inc., 1991.

Myers, Walter Dean. Amistad: A Long Road to Freedom. Dutton Children's Books, 1998.

Siebert, Wilbur H. The Underground Railroad from Slavery to Freedom. Arno Press and the New York Times, 1968.

Turner, Ann. Nettie's Trip South. MacMillan Publishing Co., 1987.

Van Steenwyk, Elizabeth. My Name is York. Northland Publishing, 1997.

Worley, Demetrice A. and Jesse Perry, Jr. African American Literature: An Anthology of Non-fiction, Poetry, and Drama. National Textbook Company, 1996.

Bibliography *(cont.)*

Resources:

National Emancipation Association, Inc.
2314 Wheeler
Houston, Texas 77004

Juneteenth, USA
c/o Representative Al Edwards
4913 Griggs
Houston, Texas 77021

Web sites:

Avalon Project—The Emancipation Proclamation
www.yale.edu/lawweb/avalon/emancipa.htm

Harriet Tubman and The Underground Railroad for Children
www2.lhric.org/pocantico/tubman/tubman.html

Harriet Tubman
www.kn.pacbell.com/wired/fil/pages/huntharriettu.html

The Access Indiana Teaching and Learning Center
tlc.ai.org/tubman.htm

Douglass—Archives of American Public Speeches
douglass.speech.nwu.edu/

FDMCC—Photo Gallery
www.ggw.org/freenet/ffdm/gallery.htm

Frederick Douglass National Historic Site
www.nps.gov/frdo/freddoug.html

Amistad Links
www.amistad.org/

Amistad
www.courant.com/news/special/amistad/history.stm

Ability's African-American History Page
www.ability.org/africanh.html

World Book Encyclopedia Presents—The African American Journey
www.worldbook.com/fun/aajourney

Slavery
www.ssnew.slink.com/link/slavery.html

Stamp on Black History—Recipes
tqd.advanced.org/10320/Breads.htm

Answer Key

Page 11

1. immune
2. slave
3. susceptible
4. labor
5. diseases
6. lucrative
7. captured
8. merchants
9. negotiated
10. condition
11. profit
12. confinement
13. toil
14. drudgery
15. hideous
16. desolate
17. culture
18. abolish
19. rampant
20. emancipation
21. victory
22. proclamation
23. equality

Page 14

1. T	9. F
2. F	10. F
3. T	11. T
4. T	12. F
5. F	13. T
6. T	14. T
7. T	15. F
8. T	

Page 22

1. He passed away, and she was angry.
2. It meant working from dawn to way past dark.
3. She thinks they are crazy with too much time on their hands.
4. Her shoes made too much noise. She became ill.
5. It was the story of Lucy and her husband running away to be together.
6. He hates slavery. He fought with his master.
7. She used straw and dirty cotton.
8. She gave Gran her freedom.
9. Miss Elizabeth's sister, Hannah, bought Gran and Mark.
10. She met her beau, "R."
11. She set her free to let her buy Mark.
12. She was a slave for 50 years.
13. He had money to buy Harriet's freedom.
14. Mrs. Norcom was.
15. He is building a house four miles out of town.

Page 25

1. Metaphor	8. Simile
2. Metaphor	9. Simile
3. Simile	10. Simile
4. Simile	
5. Simile	
6. Simile	
7. Metaphor	

Page 34

1. Many different people of varying races and backgrounds work for the Underground Railroad.
2. The end of the line was the North where freedom could be found, often as far north as Canada.
3. Many people working together, using all they had available to them (wagons, their homes, barns, etc.) were what made the train.
4. It was the "Freedom Train" because slaves "rode" on it when they were headed for freedom.
5. It was showing that the effort of the Underground Railroad was a collective effort of many different people working together for the same goal.
6. They were breaking the laws of slavery by helping people escape to the North (In many states, it was the same as stealing property).
7. The laws of God are that all men are equal and deserve to be free, and men aren't as wise as God because the laws of slavery don't allow people to be free, but the law of God is justice for all mankind.

Page 39

1. Harriet escaped from slavery on the Underground Railroad.
2. She tied two chickens around her waist to distract him from looking at her face.
3. She waded through swamps and marshes, and she hid in wagons or buggies.
4. She would give it sleeping medicine.
5. No, he forgot about Harriet and married someone else.
6. She must have felt very sad and angry at him for forgetting about her.
7. Her brothers had been sold and were to be moved.
8. Old Rit must have felt lonely, sad, worried, and disappointed that her sons didn't come for Christmas dinner.
9. She made her parents leave all their belongings behind and drove them on a buggy until they arrived at the train station where they took the train all the way to Canada.
10. Harriet was brave, intelligent, determined, resourceful, dedicated to the cause, and caring.
11. No, Harriet cared for her parents and the elderly and spoke out for blacks' and women's rights.
12. She worked for the Underground Railroad, helped many people escape, worked as a nurse, cooked and spied during the Civil War, cared for her parents, cared for the elderly, and spoke out for blacks' and women's rights.

Page 44

1800s—Dred Scott is born.
1820—Missouri Compromise is formed.
1834—Dred Scott moves with Emerson to Illinois from Missouri.
1836—Dred Scott and Emerson live in Wisconsin.
1837—Dred Scott and Emerson move to Louisiana, and Emerson marries Eliza Sanford.
1843—Emerson dies, leaves Scott and his wife, Harriet, to Eliza Sanford.
1846—Dred and Harriet petition Missouri Court for freedom.
1850—Jury awards freedom.
1852—Case is reheard.
1853—Case is filed in U.S. Federal Court and is unsuccessful.
1856—Supreme Court Case begins.
1857—Judge rules that Dred Scott is not free.
1858—Blow takes possession of Dred and Harriet and sets them free. Scott dies in September.

Page 48

1. It freed slaves in Union-occupied states.
2. The South
3. The Union Army needed more soldiers.
4. + 5. Answer will vary.

Page 54

1. c,h,q
2. d
3. a,e,s
4. f,k
5. g,l
6. b,g,m
7. i,n
8. j,o
9. p,r,t

Page 61

1. 42 ft (13 m)
2. 120 sq ft (37 m)
3. 86 ft (26.4 m)
4. 138 sq ft (42.5 m)
5. 155 sq ft (47.6 m), 114 ft (35 m)
6. 35 x 6 ft (10.8 x 1.8 m) because the area is 210 sq ft (64.5 m)
7. Answers will vary.

Page 63

1. 35 miles
2. 45 miles
3. 20 miles
4. 100 miles
5. 2 miles every 2 hours
6. about 66 days
7. 5 miles a day
8. 45,000 miles in all
9. The next town is 45 miles away and it is Wilmington.
10. The southernmost town is Bucktown, and it is 100 miles away.